BEARS

Behavior, Ecology, Conservation

Text by Erwin A. Bauer

Photographs by Erwin and Peggy Bauer

Voyageur Press

Edited by Todd R. Berger
Interior design by Helene C. J. Anderson
Cover design by Andrea Rud
Printed in Hong Kong

Hardcover edition
98   99   00   01   02   6   5   4   3   2
Softcover edition
99   00   01   02   03   5   4   3   2   1

Library of Congress Cataloging-in-Publication Data
Bauer, Erwin A.
Bears : behavior, ecology, conservation / text by Erwin A. Bauer ;
photography by Erwin and Peggy Bauer
p. cm.
Includes bibliographical references (p. 153) and index.
ISBN 0-89658-282-5
ISBN 0-89658-428-3 (pbk.)
1. Bears—North America.   I. Bauer, Peggy.   II. Title.
QL737.C27B378   1996
599.74′446′097—dc20   96-2185
                                                          CIP

Published by Voyageur Press, Inc.
123 North Second Street, P.O. Box 338, Stillwater, MN 55082 U.S.A.
651-430-2210, fax 651-430-2211

Educators, fundraisers, premium and gift buyers, publicists, and marketing managers:
Looking for creative products and new sales ideas? Voyageur Press books are available at special discounts
when purchased in quantities, and special editions can be created to your specifications. For details
contact the marketing department at 800-888-9653.

Page 1: *Triplet cubs huddle against their brown bear
mother, as she watches for a sign of salmon spawning in the McNeil River, Alaska.*

Page 4: *Tracks of a traveling brown bear are etched
in the soft earth along the southwestern Alaska
coast.*

Facing page: *A central Alaskan grizzly bear stops
digging for ground squirrels to watch another bear
digging nearby.*

Dedication

This book is dedicated to all members of conservation clubs, foundations, institutes, and coalitions that work so hard to secure a place for all bears to live on forever.

Contents

Introduction

Late on a golden afternoon in mid-July, I slipped off my heavy backpack to rest, standing knee-deep in wildflowers of an alpine meadow. For three days I had been hiking the Teton Crest Trail, sometimes in warm sunshine, but just as often in a cold rain. Now I was on my way home, and I was weary. In traveling better than twenty miles (32 km), I had seen only two other hikers. Here where the trail bisected the meadow was a perfect spot to rest complaining muscles. Maybe I dozed. It was easy to drift off while stretched out comfortably on the ground with my head resting on the backpack.

Suddenly, I was wide awake. I had company. As I sat upright, I saw two small black bear cubs wrestling and romping a short distance away in the lavender and yellow wildflowers. Then I heard shuffling directly behind me and turned to see a shaggy adult black bear approaching. Undoubtedly, this was the mother.

The conventional wisdom is never to come between a mother bear and her cubs. Inadvertently, I had done exactly that. There were no trees to climb, so I briefly considered running. But I knew that running was the dumbest thing I could do; black bears can run much faster than people. Fortunately, that bear circled past me not fifty feet (15 m) distant, turning her head my way but still not seeming to notice me at all. She went directly to her cubs.

While my pulse slowly returned to normal, the three bears gamboled across the field in a way I had never seen black bears behave before. I stood still until the bears reached the far edge of the meadow, and then I quickly slipped into my backpack straps and hurried away down the steep path toward the Death Canyon trailhead. In that whole summer of hiking the spectacular backcountry of Grand Teton National Park—in fact, for several summers—my encounter with that black bear family was the highlight.

A resting black bear on a warm summer day.

BEARS AND PEOPLE

Throughout North American history, bears have furnished the human population with highlights and headaches, folklore and fear, curiosity and admiration, and tales both tragic and humorous. Bears have often been portrayed as adversaries in our so-called mission to "tame" our land. Bears were, or somehow seemed to be, the bane of our pioneer forefathers, and for a long time humans used any means possible, from traps and guns to poisons and aircraft harassment, to get rid of them. Fortunately, that seems to be changing. More and more people think of a bear in other ways: as Smoky, the symbol of forest fire prevention; as Brother Bear; as one of the great game animals; or simply as one of the most interesting creatures to stalk across the land.

Over the decades, we have named countless places for bears. Consider the well-known Beartooth Highway route into Yellowstone and the Absaroka-Beartooth Wilderness, which I can see looming beyond my back door. There are hundreds of Bear and Grizzly lakes and creeks from Nova Scotia to California. Bear Lake National Wildlife Refuge is in Utah. I think also of Spotted Bear Ranger Station, Grizzly Peak, the Bearpaw Mountains and Bear Paw Battlefield, Bearmouth and Beartrap Canyons, even Bear Ass Gulch, all of these in Montana alone. Our admiration for the animal's prowess is evident, given that more high school and college team nicknames are adopted from bears than anything else. In addition, we have bears on the professional level, including the Boston Bruins, the Chicago Bears, the Chicago Cubs, and the Vancouver Grizzlies.

EVOLUTION OF THE BEAR

There still is much to learn about bears. Sadly, we may not develop complete knowledge of this wonderful

An adult brown bear pauses in its pursuit of salmon, perhaps just to stretch, where an unnamed Alaskan salmon stream enters tidewater.

animal before the last one disappears from the face of the earth. Even the origin of the bear is mysterious. Most likely, bears evolved about thirty-five to forty million years ago from a family of meat-eating, tree-climbing mammals known as miacids that lived in what is today Europe. This family also included ancestors of wild dogs, such as wolves and foxes, as well as raccoons. Miacids developed canine teeth, used to tear and eat flesh.

Scientists believe that early miacids had small brains. They did not need to be smart to catch abundant and not very intelligent prey. But what followed, according to scientists, was an evolutionary arms race, so to speak, in which both the miacids and their prey developed larger brains, the better to outwit one another.

Perhaps the oldest known bear-offshoot of the miacid family was *Ursavus elemensis*, which roamed Europe about twenty million years ago and was the size of a beagle. Since that time, bears have grown greatly in bulk and certainly in range. Many species lived for a while and then became extinct.

The first bear in the same genus as North Ameri-can bears are classified, *Ursus,* appeared about 2.5 million years ago, and was the first bear to be hunted by humans.

Skeletal remains of another ancient bear, in fact great piles of bones from *Ursus spelaus,* have been discovered deep in caves in Austria and the Swiss Alps. The remains date from ten thousand to over forty thousand years ago. Some of these skeletons reveal that the animals were killed by stone axes, but a change of habitat and climate may also have been a factor.

The ancestors of our black bear, *Ursus americanus,* and our grizzly and brown bear, *Ursus arctos,* arrived on this continent about 1.5 million years ago from Eurasia by crossing the Bering Land Bridge that once connected northeastern Siberia with Alaska. A third species, *Arctodus simus* or the short-faced bear, also made the crossing. This bear also evolved from the miacids but was significantly different enough to be classified under a separate genus. The short-faced bear was the largest of the migrants, and we know about it mostly from remains unearthed in California's Rancho La Brea tar pits, where many animals were trapped and died. The most recently evolved bear is the polar

Above: *The hiking trail to Mt. Washburn's summit in Yellowstone National Park was temporarily closed when this male grizzly approached too near to parties of hikers. Eventually it moved elsewhere.*

Facing page: *With a fresh-run salmon in its mouth, a brown bear splashes to shore at Hallo Bay, Alaska to eat its catch.*

bear, *Ursus maritimus*. It is thought to have branched from other *Ursus* bears around one hundred thousand years ago.

APPEARANCE

To most people, the bears of today (members of the family Ursidae) look pretty much alike in body shape, although not as much in size and color. Their skeletons are similar to those of their distant relatives, the wild dogs. All bears have powerful bodies, relatively short legs and tails, and rounded ears. Their eyes are small and are often hard to see, except in direct sunlight. Their dense, heavy pelts give the false impression that bears are clumsy or ponderous animals, but exactly the opposite is true: Bears are very fast afoot and agile. They can run thirty miles per hour (48 kph), covering forty-four feet (13 m) in a second, which is faster than an Olympic sprinter. Bears also are strong swimmers. The lips of bears are not connected to their gums, unlike in other carnivores (which bears are classified as, despite their varied diet).

Bears resemble humans in many ways. They have five toes on each foot and are plantigrade, which means they walk with feet flat on the ground. In fact, they are pigeon-toed and can easily stand up on hind legs. An early Native American name for the grizzly bear is translated as "the beast that walks like a man." All bear toes have long, curving claws that are nonretractable but can be used somewhat like human fingers for such tasks as stripping berries from bushes.

The teeth of bears grow slowly throughout their lives. Careful examination of the jaws can give biologists a good idea about the animal's health and history. Faint rings (like the rings on tree trunks) reveal the age of the individual.

BEARS OF THE WORLD

Altogether there are nine species of bears living on earth today, inhabiting four of the continents, North America, South America, Europe, and Asia. The bears of North America are doing relatively well, but bears on other continents are not faring nearly as well. The sun bear, *Helarctos malayanus*, smallest of all Ursidae, inhabits the dwindling tropical forests of the Malay Peninsula, Myanmar, Thailand, Borneo, Java, and Sumatra. *Melursus ursinus*, the sloth bear, is a black,

shaggy, sometimes surly species of India, Nepal, and Sri Lanka where it barely clings to existence in the face of shrinking habitat and intense hunting pressure. The same is true of the Andean or spectacled bear, *Tremarctos ornatus*, of the extreme northwestern South American highlands. The Asiatic black or moon bear, *Selenarctos thibetanus*, once claimed a wide range in northern India and Pakistan, Tibet, Manchuria, and the Japanese islands of Honshu and Shikoku. But no one really knows its true status or numbers today. Conservationists around the world are making a great effort to save the giant panda, *Ailuropoda melanoleauca*, and to preserve the small sanctuaries in which a few hundred still survive in late 1990s China.

Eurasian brown bears, *Ursus arctos arctos,* still live in scattered habitats from Finland eastward to Russia's Kamchatka Peninsula just across the Bering Sea from Alaska. This bear is closely related to the North American grizzly and brown bears. Eurasian brown bears may be abundant in some reserves in far eastern Siberia, and at one time they also ranged far south into Asia. During a trip through Iran before the country's

Above: *The polar or white bear which ranges along the Arctic coasts of Canada and Alaska is believed to have branched from other North American bears about 100,000 years ago.*

Facing page: *A Yellowstone grizzly, which may have been digging into a rotting tree stump for insects, glances quickly at the photographer before disappearing.*

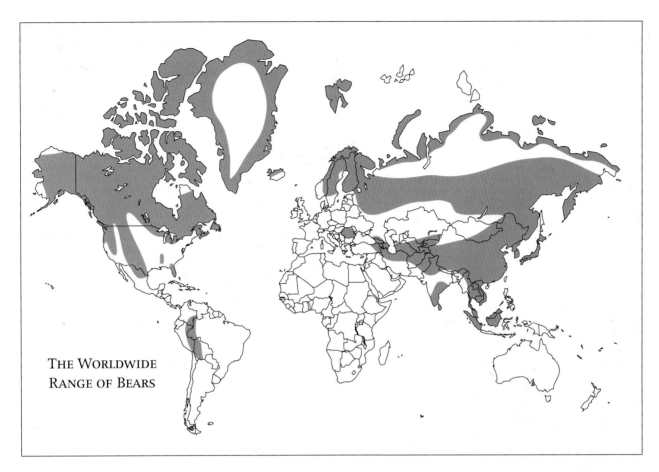

THE WORLDWIDE
RANGE OF BEARS

terrible upheaval in the 1970s, I saw two Eurasian brown bears in the northern mountains of the country. They may not survive there today.

This book will focus on the North American grizzlies, browns, and blacks, which, on a mountainside far away or in the dappled light of a forest, may not be easy to tell apart. According to one story, which may have originated with the first humans who crossed the Bering Land Bridge along with the first bears, there is one sure-fire way to distinguish them. First, you wait until the animal chases or charges you. Next you climb the nearest tree. If the bear climbs the tree to catch you, it's a black. If it shakes you out, it's a grizzly. We will begin our adventure now with the one that climbs up to catch you, but to tell the truth such behavior is extremely rare.

Facing page, top: *Especially in springtime, when vegetation is fresh and green, black bears like this one in Michigan forage almost continually, day and night.*

Facing page, bottom: *Afognak Island, Alaska. A young brown bear arrives too late at the carcass of a sea lion, washed ashore and eaten by other larger bears.*

Black Bears

Despite numbering an estimated 450,000 across Canada and the United States (and a few stragglers in northern Mexico), black bears are elusive, retiring animals difficult to see in the wild. A few national parks offer slightly better chances to meet one, but next to the mountain lion, the black bear is likely the shyest of all of our large mammals.

It is not surprising that black bears avoid humans. Soon after the British waded ashore at Plymouth Rock and the Spanish began permanent communities in southern California, the new inhabitants organized "to cleare the settlments of the wilde beares," as one Pilgrim wrote to relatives in England. Before the Europeans came, killing a bear was considered an act of bravery and qualified the killer for membership in the council of chiefs of many American Indian tribes. Among other Native American groups, all bears were respected and given a wide berth. However, the white settlers arriving in ever greater numbers had no such respect for the animals. Between wars and skirmishes with British redcoats and Indians, a restless young man could best prove himself by slaying a black bear, especially one that was poaching chickens or digging into vegetable gardens. Along the expanding frontier, hero worship was the reward for the best bear killer or trapper in any community. Daniel Boone and, later, Davy Crockett were among these heroes.

This early human animosity undoubtedly contributed to black bear shyness, enabling it to survive among people today. Mostly, today's bruins seem to dissolve into their forest habitat far from humans, their guns, and their biases.

Early in the morning an Alberta black bear crosses a small stream in its search for food. Riparian areas are ideal for foraging.

BLACK BEAR POPULATION AND RANGE

Not only are black bears hard to see in the wild, but they are especially difficult to census. The naturalist and writer Ernest Thompson Seton, in his *Lives of Game Animals* of 1929, calculated the black bear population at about two million before the arrival of Columbus. By the early 1990s, the species survived, in at least token numbers, in thirty of the forty-nine states (excluding Hawaii) where they originally occurred. They are numerous enough to justify hunting seasons in twenty-two or twenty-three states every year. Bears still wander in all of the Canadian provinces and territories, where they can legally be hunted.

Black bears are at home from sea level to the highest coniferous forests, as long as there is adequate food. Within the United States, most exist today in the West, as might be expected, where the largest tracts of wilderness and semi-wilderness remain, and where human populations are lowest. Washington has the most bears with an estimated thirty thousand in 1994. Numbers are also high in Oregon, Idaho, Montana, Colorado, and northern California, as well as across Canada north of the human population belt along the U.S.

Above: *A southern black bear explores around the fringe of a cypress slough in northern Florida, searching for edibles.*

Facing page: *The toppled trunk of a tree in northern Minnesota might hold a bonanza of ants or other insects for this foraging black bear.*

border.

As recently as 1945, as many as twelve thousand to thirteen thousand black bears lived in the southeastern United States. They still inhabit all states in the region, but in some cases black bears just barely survive. West Virginia and Mississippi were believed to have fewer than twenty-five each in 1995. Arkansas, Virginia, and Georgia probably have the most, with between twelve hundred and fifteen hundred each. The bears of the Southeast have less than 25 percent of their original range left, and the remaining lands are a scattered patchwork of isolated tracts of mature forests and swamplands. There is simply not enough quality habitat remaining to support large black bear populations.

Although most southeastern bears are fairly safe on federal lands and have no natural enemies, they nonetheless feel the squeeze of too-rapid population growth. That is especially true in Florida, which was once prime bear country. Now condominiums dominate the east coast beaches where bears once hunted for sea turtle eggs. Bears also foraged over the tropical hardwood hammocks where metropolitan Miami now sprawls, and formerly roamed the now paved-over Florida Keys. As late as 1958, a bear wandered into the center of then sleepy Naples and was attacked by local dogs. It had to be shot, because people were afraid of it. In addition, oil and gas exploration have greatly diminished bear range in Louisiana and the other Gulf states. Hundreds of miles of roads were built through cypress forests to connect oil rigs. Other forests were cleared for pipelines.

The larger the human population and the greater the activity level, the more chances there are for encounters between bears and people. Consider one special case in Texas. In 1944, Big Bend National Park was established in a remote, rugged area along the Rio Grande River at the Mexican border. Black bears were rarely if ever seen there until suddenly in 1988 some twenty-six sightings were reported in the Chisos Mountains section of the park. By 1993, with full protection from hunting inside the park, over five hundred sightings were recorded, and it became necessary to install bear-resistant dumpsters and trash cans in campgrounds. Bear damage still occurred, but it was manageable—until the bears began to wander

outside park boundaries. In September 1994, one sow with twin cubs was alleged to have killed fifteen goats and sheep. A battle with neighboring ranchers began. It is still unsettled. Now ranchers usually shoot these animals that they regard as vermin. Black bears do not have a bright future in the Lone Star State, where 97 percent of the land is privately owned and anything that can possibly eat livestock is regarded as a plague.

Black bears once inhabited all of the Northeast (and may have been abundant) except the coastal regions of Rhode Island and Massachusetts. By about 1900, land clearing and human settlements had eliminated most of them. But during the past half-century, some fifteen million acres of abandoned, low-grade farmland has slowly reverted to forest, some of which is again becoming suitable bear habitat. The bear population in Maine is estimated today at 20,000 to 21,000, the largest population in any state east of the Mississippi River. About 6,300 roam Pennsylvania's bear range and about 4,100 live in New York. Bears are fairly common in sections of western Massachusetts, New Hampshire, and Vermont, but are threatened in these states by a new surge of land development. Very small numbers survive in Maryland, New Jersey, and Connecticut, and the species is gone altogether from Delaware and Rhode Island.

In the Great Lakes region, about seventy thousand square miles (182,000 sq km) of primary bear range extends across northern Michigan, Wisconsin, and Minnesota. Habitat loss continues to be a problem across the Midwest, as suburbs continually expand outward into bear range and timber cutting is accelerated. But there is some good news for black bears in this area. Although the three states do not manage public lands explicitly for bears, they do manage extensively for whitetailed deer (which are valuable economically), and thus also improve much bear habitat. About twelve thousand bears live in Minnesota. The populations are smaller in Wisconsin and Michigan.

I met my first midwestern black bear at daybreak one still, cold morning in 1950 while sitting on a deer stand in Michigan's Upper Peninsula. Through wide, young eyes, that bruin seemed much bigger than it probably was. The animal walked silently around the fringe of a balsam swamp directly toward a very shaken and surprised hunter. Do I shoot it, I wondered? Suddenly the animal detected me and stopped. Just as quickly, it disappeared from sight, but I could hear that bear cracking through the thin crust of ice that

covered a nearby swamp as it bounded away.

FOLLOWING THE BLACK BEAR

For far too long, all that we knew about black bears we learned while looking over the barrel of a rifle. That day in Michigan, for example, I learned that this animal, weighing more than I did, could move through a forest quietly, almost ghostlike, sense danger, and then instantly vanish. But in recent times, we have acquired much more scientific information about this interesting species, thanks to the research of a few dedicated bear biologists. Among the best (and best known) of them is Dr. Lynn Rogers, founder of the Black Bear Institute in Ely, Minnesota.

Without interruption and with little distraction for almost three decades, Rogers has been studying black bears in northern Minnesota's Superior National Forest. He has made enough footprints to take him around the world several times, has crawled head-first into more than 450 winter bear dens, has collared

drugged animals, and has poked through piles of bear feces. For Lynn Rogers, the word research often translates into long hours of hard labor, but he maintains a pleasant, enthusiastic personality and a great affection for his subjects. A colleague once said that Rogers sees the northern forests through bear-colored glasses. Friends call him "Mr. Bear." So maybe the best way to look at the natural history of *Ursus americanus* is through Lynn Rogers's eyes—or through the immense amount of data he collected while based at the North Central Experiment Station of the U.S. Forest Service in Saint Paul.

We begin our inquiry with the question most asked of Lynn Rogers: "Are black bears really dangerous?" Rogers's answer is a definite no. He has invaded dens to tranquilize grouchy old bruins and draw their blood; fitted hundreds of bears with radio collars and taken their temperatures; and chased, treed, and captured their cubs for study. Despite all of this close exposure to black bears, he has never been attacked. In fact, one day he accidentally fell on top of a mother bear, kicking her in the teeth and striking her head with his camera, and the animal still did not bite.

Though he has never been attacked, Rogers certainly has been tested. Different bears use distinct threat gestures, from snorting and snapping teeth to extending lips and lunging, but rarely are these followed by a real attack. Females most aggressively defend their cubs, but there is a limit. They try to escape danger with the cubs, or without them as a last resort. Since early in this century there have been thousands of close encounters between black bears and people in North America, but fewer than fifty unprovoked attacks have been reported and only eighteen of these were fatal—a remarkable statistic. Contrast those long odds with the perils of walking sidewalks in any large city in the United States or to driving on busy highways. As Rogers tells me, a person could spend a lifetime exploring in the best bear habitat and be safer than strolling alone just one evening in most urban parks.

Since his college days at Michigan State, Rogers has tracked black bears from trucks, canoes, snowmobiles, cross-country skis, aircraft, afoot, and sometimes on hands and knees. Altogether he has intensively followed 128 different animals; studied one

Above: *Although there have been fatal encounters with black bears in the past, chances of an attack are very, very small. But keep a safe distance anyway.*

Facing page: *Black bears share this exquisite fall scene year round in Grand Teton National Park, Wyoming, with grizzlies, elk, moose, and mule deer.*

extended family group, or clan, for four generations; and ear-tagged 350 animals of all ages, including one that reached twenty-one years of age. Keeping track of any animal that can run like a deer, climb trees, and swim across lakes is exhausting work, but the work of dedicated bear researchers such as Dr. Lynn Rogers results in extremely valuable scientific information, much of which appears in this book.

MATING

Female black bears begin to breed when they reach two and a half or three and a half years of age. Males can also mate at this age, but older males do most of the breeding. Copulation takes place some time between early June and the end of July, the date depending primarily on latitude: Black bears breed earlier in the southern parts of the range and later in the north. Black bears can be promiscuous, and many if not most mate with more than one sow or boar each season. After mating, males ignore the females and their offspring. The boars live solitary bachelor lives until the next breeding season comes around. Both males and females spend the rest of the summer wandering widely in fairly well-defined territories and eating as much as they can. The object is to accumulate enough fat to sustain them through the oncoming winter.

The fertilized ova in the female grow very little during the summer and early fall. By the onset of winter the embryos are only about one inch (2.5 cm) long. After a gestation period of 200 to 210 days, one, two, or occasionally three cubs are born. Litters of four and even five cubs are exceedingly rare but are not unknown. Most of the cubs in a geographic region are born at roughly the same time. In colder, northern regions they are usually born in underground hibernation sites, but some sites may be above ground, under (or inside) tree deadfalls. The survival rate is low when the den is not warm. In the South the sows use remote, snug dens above or below ground.

HIBERNATION

Hibernation has always been the most mysterious, most intriguing aspect of the lives of black bears, as well as those of grizzly and brown bears. Winter dormancy can last as long as seven months in parts of Alaska to only a short snooze in Florida or Louisiana. In the North, hibernation sites are often caves or crevices underground. Snow may seal off the opening to the den completely. In the South, a bear may simply hibernate in snug beds excavated beneath deadfalls or in hillsides. But regardless of geographic location, bears are often creative about where they choose to sleep through the winter. In bitterly cold Yellowstone Park, a bear once denned over winter beneath the loading platform of a storage warehouse at Old Faithful. In Louisiana, a female twice bore cubs in an abandoned root cellar built before the Civil War.

A bear begins the search for its own den or hibernation site when the days begin to grow short and fall's food supplies have been depleted. After finding a suitable site and once asleep, the hibernators do not emerge to eat or drink, nor do they urinate or defecate. Body temperature falls and the metabolism rate drops markedly. Cubs come into the world, nurse, and grow in the darkness of the winter den, perhaps without their mothers even being aware of it. On very rare occasions, such as during prolonged and abnormal warm spells, bears have stirred from their lethargy and moved about outside their winter dens. Some Boy Scouts on a winter hike in January along the Little Bushkill Creek in New York State came across a "big" bear rolling in the snow. A week later another "big" bear crossed the ice of Lake Wallenpaupack in northeastern Pennsylvania in full view of several ice fishermen.

Even though a bear's kidneys shut down completely during hibernation, the animal is not poisoned by the urea that kidneys normally filter from the blood. Instead, the urea is reabsorbed from the bladder and somehow is used to produce protein and preserve muscle tissue during the long sleep. A bear might lose up to a third of its body weight during a hibernation. Scientists have long speculated that if the chemistry that triggers this phenomenon could be isolated, they might be able to better treat humans with kidney failure or other renal disorders.

This black cub in Washington, which is almost four months old, might have siblings which are either the same or another color.

MOTHER AND CUBS

At birth the eyes of cubs are closed, and they have only a very thin coat of fine, black hair. Each cub weighs around a half-pound (0.23 kg). Their eyes open in a month or so, but cubs examined in their natal dens do not seem to have good vision, probably because it is not necessary until the mothers "awaken" and begin to move about in late March or April. At that time, when they are two months or more old, the cubs each weigh about five pounds (2.27 kg). They continue to nurse for some time, but throughout their first summer the cubs gradually eat more and more of the same natural foods their mothers are eating.

Anyone able to observe the antics of wild black bear cubs is very lucky. There is always a good bit of sibling rivalry between twins, and their playful romping can become very rough. But their mother does not intervene. Cubs also make a variety of sounds from grunting and woofing, to humming, whining, and moaning that seems almost human. They learn which foods to eat, what sights and sounds to fear, and how to behave in general by following the example of their mother. Growth, even survival, depends on the skill and experience of their full-time teacher.

Most black bear cubs will spend their first full winter in the hibernation den with their mother. Some-

Excellent climbers at an early age, this cub explores a tree toppled by forest fires in Yellowstone. It is probably licking ants on the trunk.

Bears in the Air

Research biologist Harry Carriles of Montana's Glacier National Park got the surprise of his life in the winter of 1980 while searching for a radio-collared sixteen-and-a-half-year-old female. He finally located her in her den, not underground, but in the cavity of a tall larch tree, seventy feet (21 m) above the ground. He climbed an adjacent tree to double-check his radio signals. There was no mistake: Carriles found three bears in that lofty den, the female and two cubs. Carriles still wonders how, in spring, the tiny cubs reached the ground. Did they climb down or did the mother carry them?

time during their second spring, when some may weigh one hundred pounds (45 kg), they gradually wander away from their mother to seek a territory and a life of their own.

Black bear cubs are capable tree climbers. Though they can still climb as adults, the older and heavier black bears become, the poorer their climbing ability. For adults there is also less need to climb to escape danger. In Yellowstone Park, I once watched a precocious cub repeatedly climb trees to escape the discipline of a mother that had grown too heavy and perhaps too old to follow.

THE TERRITORIAL BLACK BEAR

In some parts of North America, the home ranges of black bears are better defined and defended than in other areas. Each bear seems to have a built-in contour map of its territory, which it marks by defecating and by clawing or biting tree trunks. These signs probably are well recognized by other bears. For three summers what was almost certainly the same bear claw-marked several trees on our property in Montana, until it was unaccountably shot by a neighbor whose only explanation was that he "didn't really like bears."

In Minnesota's vast North Woods, Lynn Rogers determined that black bear sows had home ranges of from two to six square miles (5–16 sq km), a territory that they often defend fiercely. Male bears roam over much larger ranges of from twenty to sixty square miles (52–156 sq km), or even more. Areas this large are much more difficult to patrol and defend.

Occasionally, when flying a light aircraft over a certain bear territory, Rogers could tell from radio signals when a female was trying to invade another

female's territory. Most often the resident bear would chase the intruder away, but sometimes serious fights would result. On one occasion a resident female threw an intruder out of a tree to its death.

DIET

Despite the fact that they evolved from pure carnivores and that they, like all bears, are classified under the order Carnivora, *Ursus americanus* has become an omnivore that under ordinary circumstances eats very little fresh meat in the wild.

The most common foods of a black bear are new green grasses early in the season, other green plants, leaves and tender buds, roots, fruits, berries, and nuts (especially acorns). In Glacier National Park, black bears do not touch sweetvetch, which is plentiful and which grizzly bears relish. But both gorge on cow-parsnip, a fast-growing, high-protein, leafy member of the carrot family and one of the first foods available

each spring. Black bears, in fact, may be responsible for the wide distribution of cow-parsnip; the seeds digested and passed through a bear germinate better than those that simply fall to the ground.

Especially in the western United States, adult bears will strip the bark from some coniferous trees, munch on the soft inner layer, and nibble on the leaking tree trunk. This practice can girdle and kill such trees as cedars and firs—a consequence that does not endear bears to foresters.

But black bears have not totally forsaken their carnivorous roots. Some black bears—a very few, probably—have learned to target deer fawns early each summer, before the fawns are able to follow their mothers. Most black bears will dig the kits out of any fox den they find or eat ground-nesting birds and their eggs. A few in the eastern United States try to excavate dens for the woodchucks inside.

Joe Kimpson, hunting near Saranac Lake, New

A black bear's vision is much better than the small eyes might indicate. Its nose may be as keen as any animal's.

York, during the spring bear season, shot a three-hundred-pound (136-kg) male that was feeding on a bear cub. In fact, instances of cannibalism have been noted almost everywhere in bear range.

In southeastern Alaska, black bears appear on certain salmon spawning streams and gorge on the protein bonanza during the short periods when the fish are "running." They will also go after other species of fish. In Ontario's Nipigon region, just north of Thunder Bay on Lake Superior, I watched a young black bear trying unsuccessfully to catch suckers spawning in a small, shallow stream. In addition, most bears seem unable to resist climbing bee trees to reach the honey, and they will endure terrible stinging to get as much as they can. Black bears will also lap up swarming insects or their larvae. However, many, if not most, wilderness black bears spend summer after summer without the taste of red meat, either fresh or carrion. Black bears are primarily vegetarians, although some seem to eat anything that is biodegradable, plus some materials that are not.

Starvation does occur, especially among very young bears, when berry and nut crops fail. One young, hungry male in Maine that tried to capture a porcupine was all too typical. When found by hikers, his muzzle was so infested with quills and infected that he could no longer eat. The bear was saved by a veterinarian who tranquilized him, removed the quills, treated the infection, and fed him for a few weeks until he regained his health and could be released. Most often, starvation is a subtle thing, detected only when a bear population fails at the same time food crops fail. Scavengers usually find the starved bodies before researchers do.

If nothing else, black bears are resourceful. A fishing guide in Georgia's Okefenokee Swamp told me of a black bear that invaded a heron and egret rookery during the spring nesting period. This bruin shook dead nest trees until the young, still flightless birds fell out. The bear then ate the chicks. To reach more chicks, the bear climbed the nest trees after them, until one dead tree toppled under the bear's weight. Undeterred, the bear quickly pounced on the young herons that were dislodged in the crash.

Commercial apiarists are not exactly wild about black bears, which can quickly make a shambles of clusters of hives. In many states, especially in the South, fish and game departments and agriculture extension agents offer plans for building bear-proof, platformed bee-keeping facilities, featuring hot electrical wires and chemicals. Even so, a few super-smart bears manage to get inside these "maximum-security" hives each summer. So great is their taste for honey that, in Michigan, black bears have been electrocuted when they mistook the buzzing of rheostats at the top of rural power poles for beehives and climbed the poles seeking a sweet snack.

Nor are some commercial fishermen enchanted with the black bears' annual "catch" of salmon on some southeastern Alaska coastal streams. They regard the bears as competition. On the few occasions when I saw black bears fishing, they did not seem to be as skillful as Alaskan brown bears. In studies at one site, Olsen Creek, biologist George Frame estimated that a changing cast of several bears altogether caught and ate about 10 percent of the unspawned chum and pink salmon entering the creek. Ten percent does not seem like a high toll of fish to me, especially when the aesthetics are considered. Bear watching and photography on coastal streams becomes more popular every year, and visitors pay well for the chance to participate.

THE LURE OF CARRION

Despite their predominantly vegetarian diet, most bears cannot resist the lure of carrion, whether the source is a natural casualty, such as a winter-killed deer or elk; a road kill; or a bait set out by humans to tempt bears into range, either to be shot—or studied.

Lynn Rogers used baiting, under carefully controlled conditions far from human dwellings, to better examine the Superior National Forest bears. By placing food on scales outside a cabin-laboratory at the Kawishiwi River, he was able for the first time to weigh live bears whenever they regularly came to feed. Eventually he was able to closely approach most of the nine bears he weighed and to affix radio collars to three. He could then monitor the radio signals and follow on foot through the woods.

There are some problems, though, with baiting, even when used for important and revealing scientific research. Baiting for any purpose must not be attempted by anyone who is unfamiliar with bear behavior, who is not physically fit, and who is not authorized to do such work. There is too much risk of personal injury. Also, baiting might very well habituate bears to seek human food elsewhere, by visiting garbage dumps or breaking into rural homes and camps. Too many black bears are already hooked on the rural garbage dumps across the northern Great Lakes region, where a good many are shot. There is also the possibility of breeding contempt—of bears losing their natural fear of humans when they are regularly fed. Bears that break into homes or that seem to be dangerous will eventually have to be dispatched.

Among Rogers's most important discoveries from years of radio-tracking was that black bear society is matriarchal. Mothers seem to divide up and share their territories with their daughters. The result can become a dynasty that goes on for generations, until overcrowding destroys it.

Above: *A young black bear samples ripening mountain ash berries while wallowing in a small pond. Now in fall is the time to eat and fatten up for winter.*

Facing page: *This bruin is marking its territory by standing erect and making claw marks on a small tree trunk.*

In addition, natural disasters, such as long droughts or failures of berry or other principal food crops, can drive many bears to wander far from their home ranges. A long, too-dry period can cause a mass movement, as it did in 1985 when thousands of black bears from Ontario invaded Minnesota and Wisconsin. The result was a frightened human population and enough damage that hundreds of invaders—as well as resident bears—were shot. The bear population fell to an all-time low in the region, but has since recovered.

PELAGE

The bodies of black bears are protected and insulated by two kinds of body hair. The soft, dense underfur functions primarily as the main insulator against cold. The guard hair, which is longer and coarser than the underfur, also insulates but serves other purposes as well. The guard hair repels water, keeping the underfur dry. Raising, or erecting, guard hairs also conveys the bear's mood to other bears, the same way some other animals use odors or pheromones to communicate fear, aggression, dominance, or sexual readiness to others of the same species.

Black bears shed both guard hairs and underfur annually. The shedding begins in late spring, in May or earlier in the Southeast and June elsewhere. The shedding is gradual, but there is a period in summer when a bear looks very shaggy or even mangy as the old hair crop falls out. Long ago, some Native American hunters were able to track black bears in summer by following the faintest trail of shed hair. By late August in the far north, the underfur has grown back, and the guard hair usually is restored by the first frost. By the time fall gives way to winter, a healthy black bear's pelage is sleek, dense, and heavy, affording enough protection for the animal to survive the winter, either above or below ground.

COLORATION

In North America no native mammal exists in so many color phases as the "black" bear. Seven or eight of every ten are black, usually with a small white or cream throat patch. The farther east in the United States and Canada, the more likely a black bear is to be black. Moving westward the percentage of rich,

Above: *Bear country in the southeastern United States is often swampland shared with wading birds such as this great blue heron. Bears have been seen taking chicks from trees in heron rookeries.*

Right: *Some black bears will catch and eat young deer fawns whenever and wherever they find them. A few become expert at hunting fawns.*

The Prize

In the northern part of Yellowstone National Park, a car struck a mule deer on the winding highway that connects the park headquarters at Mammoth with Gardiner, Montana, the park's northern gateway town. The crippled deer managed to drag itself to the Gardiner River, which closely parallels the road here, but finally fell dead in the middle of the current. Black bears don't frequent this part of the park, but somehow, probably using its remarkable sense of smell, a bear quickly found the deer and dragged the carcass onto the far bank. There, for almost five days, the bear enjoyed a banquet of carrion.

While more and more photographers gathered with telephoto lenses, and curious tourists caused traffic jams on the road overlooking the river, the bear chased away coyotes, ravens, and magpies that tried to share the windfall. When the bear wasn't actually feeding, it slept on top of or just beside its prize, which the bear had covered with vegetation. Occasionally, a magpie would manage to spear a morsel before the bear woke up. Altogether, it's estimated that the bear dined on and finished 125 to 150 pounds (57–68 kg) of meat in four and a half days, or about 30 pounds (14 kg) per day. The bear essentially ate the entire deer. All the while that bear seemed not to notice the countless people who stopped to watch.

Above: *In Yellowstone, this bear has dragged the carcass of a mule deer (injured in a car collision) to the bank of the Gardiner River. The bear remained with the carcass for days until all was eaten.*

chocolate-brown (the second most common color) bears increases. A black bear's pelage might be any shade of brown, including cinnamon, tan, and even straw-colored. It is possible that every cub in a single litter may be a different color, although black or brown hues are the most common. Many black bears tend to look grizzled around the muzzle and flanks in extreme old age. It is most noticeable on the very black individuals, when seen at a distance in a strong back- or side-light. This grizzling can make a black bear somewhat resemble its larger cousin, the grizzly bear.

One theory, Gloger's Rule, about animal coloration is worth repeating here. Among warm-blooded mammals, dark or black pigments are most prevalent in humid areas, while red and yellow pigments are more prevalent in drier areas, such as the West. Since brown- or cinnamon-phase black bears are better able to tolerate the sun's heat due to their lighter pelage, they can feed longer each day in more open habitat. They can therefore gain weight faster, produce cubs at an earlier age, and have multiple births more often than black-colored black bears. So, according to Gloger's Rule, in the drier, more open western environment, the lighter bear's tolerance to heat gives some a selective advantage over darker bears.

The most striking color phase of the black bear, in this case a separate subspecies, is that of the pure white or cream-colored bears called ghost or Kermode bears (*Ursus americanus kermodei*), named after Francis Kermode, director of the Royal British Columbia Museum. These bears live on Princess Royal Island and the adjacent mainland of British Columbia. Ghost bears are not albinos, which usually occur where there is too much inbreeding, but simply a different color phase. Kermodes compose about 10 to 15 percent of the 130 or so bears living within the Kermode bears' range. Long mistaken for polar bears, and sometimes referred to as spirit bears by coastal Indians, they are the products of a double recessive gene.

Kermode bears were almost unknown, except to Indians and fishermen, until recent decades. They live along with black-phase gray wolves in a dense primeval forest, often drenched with rain and shrouded in fog, that has changed very little since the last Ice Age. (It is doubly interesting that in this one place occur unusual color phases of both bears and wolves—one

lighter than usual, and one darker. It is probably due to a population that sees little infusion of new blood due to geographical isolation.) As I write in 1995, a battle about the future of Princess Royal Island is brewing over the provincial government's lunatic plans to clear-cut those ancient, priceless forests. If the forests go, so will the spirit bears. Forever.

Another uniquely colored black bear is the blue or glacier bear (*Ursus americanus emmonsii*). The glacier bear ranges from northern British Columbia along the coast of southeastern Alaska into the Yukon. Peggy and I were able to photograph one of these bears near Yakutat in southeastern Alaska. In the dim light of a still misty morning, the animal seemed to be slate-gray in color among the wet, green underbrush it prowled. Others have described it as bluish-silver, pewter, woodsmoke, or iron-colored.

SIZE

If you spend some time wherever "bear" people gather, in a forest camp among bear hunters or at a meeting of the Great Bear Foundation in Bozeman, Montana, you soon suspect there is no such thing as a small bear. Bears are always described as bigger, much bigger, than they actually are.

But black bears are the smallest of North American bears. They seldom reach 400 or 450 pounds (181–204 kg) or an overall length of five and a half feet (1.7 m), measured from nose tip to tail tip with the animal lying on its back. Continent wide, the average black bear weighs about 230 pounds (104 kg), a little more in the northern part of the range, a little less in the South. Males average one-fourth to one-fifth larger than females of the same age living in the same habitat. The weight of any bruin can be much greater in late fall, after bulking up for hibernation, than in early spring, when they emerge from a winter's sleep.

Bears that frequent garbage sources can be considerably larger than same-aged bears in their wild habitat. Biologist Lynn Rogers once sedated and weighed a Minnesota bear that had spent the summer rummaging around a dump. It tipped the scales at 611 pounds (277 kg).

It is very difficult to pin down the absolute maximum weight a bear might reach. In 1953, Ed Strobel shot one in Vilas County, Wisconsin, that weighed

Hunting the Trophy Hunters

Craving a trophy bear can cause some ugly situations. West Virginia conservation officer G.M. Willenborg could not believe what taxidermist Doug Milton showed him one morning in 1988: the hide and head of a black bear almost twice the size of the state's average. The skull measured 23 14/16, slightly bigger than the top Utah skull, and therefore it should be a new world record. The man who brought the trophy to Milton said he had shot the bear on the final day of West Virginia's open season.

But Willenborg was suspicious and began an investigation. He found that the monster bear had been poached out of season in adjacent Lycoming County, Pennsylvania. The poacher did not have a valid hunting license in either state. Even though its hide measures an incredible eight feet (2.5 m) nose tip to tail tip, and its weight was estimated at eight hundred pounds (363 kg), the skull has been confiscated. It remains a curiosity rather than a world record as deserved, because it was not taken legally.

Above: *Although blacks are the smallest of North American bears, some individuals with access to garbage dumps, such as this one in Ontario or the one poached in Pennsylvania, can reach great size.*

Southeast Alaska is the home of the uncommon glacier bear, a black subspecies. In certain light conditions, its coat appears to be gray or gray-blue in color.

585 pounds (265 kg) dressed; that is, with entrails removed. It could have exceeded 700 pounds (318 kg) when alive. In 1986, Dana Haagenson shot a 632-pounder (287 kg), also field dressed, near Flour Lake, Minnesota, that was judged to weigh 758 pounds (344 kg) before its death. I once read about "the grandaddy of all black bears," shot in northern Wisconsin. A Green Bay newspaper account from the early 1900s claimed that the bruin weighed 802.25 pounds (364 kg), on "honest scales."

Weight, however, is neither the only nor the best way to compare or accurately measure the size of bears. The Boone and Crockett Club, custodian of North American big game trophy records, uses a system whereby the length and width of a bleached-clean bear skull are measured in inches. These two dimensions are added together for the final score. For example, the largest black bear skull ever measured came from an animal that died of old age, or was wounded by a hunter and died later, in Sanpete County, Utah, in 1975. It measured 23 10/16 inches, or points. Of the top thirty black bear trophies listed in the latest (1993) Boone and Crockett *Records of North American Big Game*, most were taken in the western United States and western Canada, and almost half of these (fourteen) in just two states, Utah and Arizona. Although black bears with the largest skull measurements also tend to be the heaviest bears, there is no absolute correlation between the two.

LIFE EXPECTANCY

How long do black bears live? I can find no statistics to support this, but almost certainly there are older bears on average in national parks and other sanctuaries than in areas with open hunting seasons. It is simply too difficult with today's technology to accurately measure bear age in the wild. We do know, however, that individual bears have survived in captivity for twenty years or more on vitamin-fortified, but unnatural, diets.

Mark Henckel, outdoor editor of the *Billings Gazette*, in Montana, told the story of one very unusual

In spring following the 1988 forest fires in Yellowstone, a black bear finds the desiccated carcass of a bull elk, but little left to eat.

animal in a 1990 column. Patrick Hill, a Crow Indian, was hunting in Montana's Pryor Mountains in October 1989, when he shot a large black bear. Later, its hide would measure six and a half feet (2 m) long, and Hill estimated its weight at six hundred pounds (272 kg). Skull measurements revealed it to be one of the largest black bears ever taken in the state. But most remarkable of all was the bear's age, twenty-five years, as determined by an examination of its teeth by Montana Fish, Wildlife and Parks personnel. Although the teeth were well worn down, the bear might have lived a few more years. As Henckel did in his column, I marvel at how long and how well this animal had managed to elude hunters. I also wonder how many cubs it sired, and I am curious about the drastic changes in the land that elderly bear had seen. For a quarter of a century, cattle, sheep, timber cutting, and increased recreational use have all taken a toll in the Pryor Mountains, and that bruin experienced it all.

NAVIGATIONAL ABILITY

Scientists are divided over the "homing" or navigational ability of black bears, as well as that of other mammals. But there is strong evidence that bears and some other species have such built-in skills. Biologists in Yellowstone and other national parks are amazed at how quickly most "problem" or "nuisance" bears that have been live-trapped and moved far away quickly find their way right back to where they were trapped. Even when moved by helicopter as far as twenty-five or thirty miles (40–48 km) to completely unfamiliar terrain, both grizzly and black bears may very soon reappear where they caused trouble in the first place. A gray wolf in a similar situation found its way 175

All bears are strong swimmers, able to cross swift-flowing rivers and to cross large lakes.

miles (282 km) back to its starting point near Barrow, Alaska. It is believed that that wolf homed in on the sound of the large jet aircraft that frequently flew near its point of origin. A different wolf, moved at the same time, traveled to another airport one hundred miles (161 km) in the wrong direction. But what about black bears?

Ursus might be able to find its way home by several means. Its sense of smell may be the keenest of any creature's on the continent. The area of nasal mucous membrane in a bear's head is several times larger than a human's. In addition, black bears are extremely intelligent. Tests conducted by animal psychologists of the University of Tennessee suggest that black bears are among the most intelligent of all native mammals. Relative to body size, their brains are the heaviest of any native carnivores. There is also plenty of evidence that they can store information. Adults seem to remember feeding places that they visited long ago as cubs with their mothers.

Lynn Rogers described the travels of one eleven-year-old Minnesota bear that he had radio-collared. During a long drought when the berry crop had also failed, "Big Mac" wandered 125 miles (201 km) from his home territory in search of food, with Rogers and an assistant following him. Traveling almost always at night, the animal made it right back to his starting point in nine days.

Researcher El Harger of Michigan's Department of Natural Resources once moved an adult female in the state's Upper Peninsula, and that bear found its way back over 142.5 unfamiliar miles (229 km). He then moved another, with a cub, that might eventually have topped that record. For two months this female traveled 43 miles (69 km) directly toward home before the cub was killed crossing a highway. Traveling alone she soon reached Keweenaw Bay on Lake Superior and the town of L'Anse, where she was shot in somebody's backyard. But she was still on track for home. This bear had covered 98 miles (158 km) altogether in sixty-six days. Black bears are remarkable animals in so many ways.

Sometimes, bears even gain weight on the road,

perhaps because of a knack for locating dumps and other unnatural food supplies. In New York's Adirondacks, a garbage dump bear that appeared dangerous was moved sixty-five miles (105 km) away. A year later it was back, but had gained almost 100 pounds (45 kg) in the interval. Another male gained 240 pounds (109 kg), moving from 322 to 562 pounds (146–255 kg), in one year. Two others, tagged and released far from an area they frequented where they were a nuisance to cabin owners, were back within three weeks, having gained 81 and 92 pounds (37 and 42 kg).

BLACK BEARS AND PEOPLE

In addition to their sweet tooth, their cunning, and their survivability, black bears have much in common with people. Both humans and bears can stand on their hind legs. A bruin's spinal column and internal organs are similar to those of a human being's. Bears have the same kind of stomach as we do, and our stomachs are also the same size. The skinned carcass of a bear looks eerily like that of *Homo sapiens*. They can solve certain problems (like most humans), defend what belongs to them, and usually know when it's wiser to retreat than fight. But despite a reputation to the contrary, bears are not nearly as homicidal as people have become.

LEARNING FROM BLACK BEARS

Most of the people who work with or have ever worked with bears—biologists, game wardens, and law enforcement specialists—develop a genuine admiration, even an affection for them. Dr. Lynn Rogers is among them. But many others also get caught up in "bear fascination."

Michigan biologist Al Erickson trapped the first of more than one hundred black bears in 1952 and was a pioneer in the field of live capture and release. In the beginning, he used only foot snares, and that was rough work. A gang of assistants had to wrestle foot-trapped bears to the ground. They would use chains and chokers until someone could sit on the animal and hold an ether cone over its muzzle until it passed out. Erickson was battered and bruised, and a few bears died from the rough handling. Two bears suffered broken jaws that had to be bolted together before release. From today's perspective, it was a primitive system.

Still, Erickson remembers those days as worthwhile and exciting. "We learned a lot, and I wouldn't trade them for anything," he told me years later when he was live-capturing and marking polar bears on the ice fields off Alaska's northwest coast. Over many years, the connection between Erickson and bears was still very strong.

Charles Jonkel of Montana, who later would also study polar and grizzly bears, has handled some six hundred bears, including numerous black bears, during nineteen years of field research. No doubt that is a record unlikely to be matched. The fact that he has emerged from all of this work intact shows his skill in his profession and is evidence that black bears are not really as dangerous as most of us think. In fact, he has stated that even sows with cubs are basically cowards that give all kinds of warning before they attack, if they attack at all.

In 1974, Dave Graber began to study the black bears in Yosemite National Park, California, and he has handled 350 different animals since then. That may be as many as a third of all the bears that lived in the Yosemite region during his research period. Today he is convinced that black bears are by far the most interesting animals in the park. He also believes that, for a while, the Yosemite population was larger than it would have been if supported by natural food alone. Granola bars, beef jerky, and other human food from backpackers afforded the protein necessary for some bears to live at unnaturally high numbers at higher than normal altitudes.

Graber and his associates invented a complex cable and pulley system that was meant to keep food packs well out of a bear's reach around campgrounds. But

Facing page, top: *After crossing an Ontario lake, a bear shakes off water before moving away into the forest.*

Facing page, bottom: *It is summer when the living is easy. This bear is grazing its way across a meadow in Great Smoky Mountains National Park, Tennessee.*

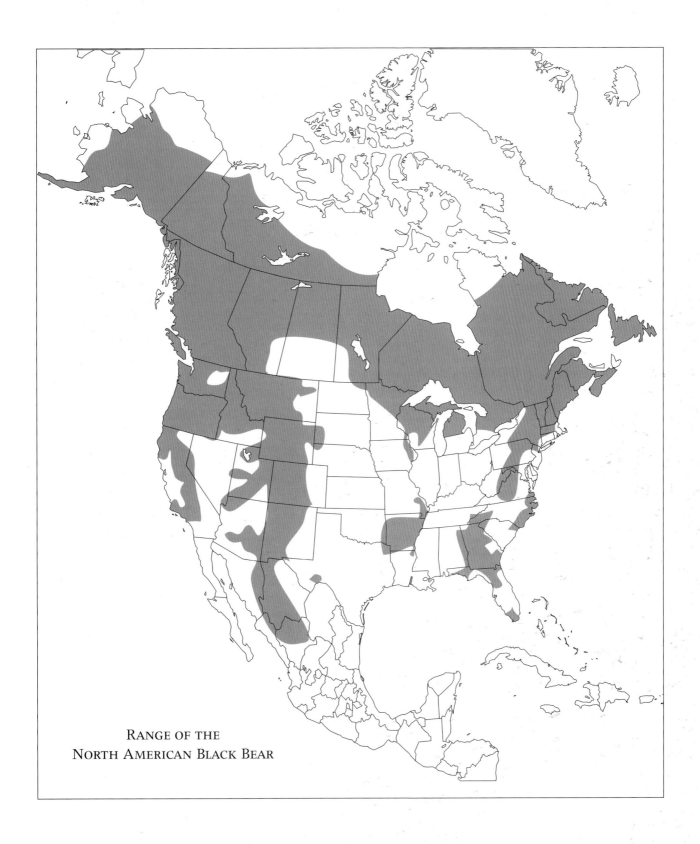

RANGE OF THE
NORTH AMERICAN BLACK BEAR

Facing page: *Solid black is the predominate coat color of a species that may be any color from almost white to black. This is an adult male.*

Right: *A few all-white black bears live on Princess Royal Island, British Columbia.* Photo © Rod Gardner

Below: *This light brown—or cinnamon—color phase was photographed on Washington's Olympic Peninsula where far more black bears are coal black.*

one clever bear soon figured out that manipulating the cable in a certain way would shake loose the backpacks, which would then drop to the ground. Other bears were quick to catch on.

Gary Alt is another busy bear biologist, whose natural habitat for many years has been Pennsylvania, often in the Pocono Mountains only about ninety miles (145 km) from New York City. He has had to evict bears that invaded summer cabins, hibernated, and gave birth under front porches. The bears broke into food freezers, which they forgot to close when they finished eating, and devoured everything from prime rib steaks and stone crabs to chocolate ice cream. One mother bear Alt "knew," broke into a kitchen, seized enough goodies to have a party, and proceeded to dine on the porch outside with her cubs. Fortunately Alt has a supply of equanimity and a sense of humor along with his scientific background.

Alt's work has exposed three common myths about black bears. First, they do not always hibernate in caves or deep dens; he has also found them sleeping in culverts beneath highways, under tree stumps, in root cavities, as well as under cabin porches. Second, cold weather alone does not drive bears into hibernation. Lack of available food does. Bears will likely ignore the cold and remain active as long as they have plenty to eat. Third, black bears, at least in Pennsylvania, do not often reuse dens or return to dens where they were born. In a ten-year study of winter denning, Alt learned that only one in twenty bears used the same den more than once.

Douglas Pierson of Washington's Department of Game is another biologist who admits to a warm feeling about bears. Once a large problem bear was acci-

dentally given an overdose of tranquilizer before being hauled away to a more remote area. When it appeared that the animal would not revive, Pierson knelt beside it and maintained a steady rhythmic pressure on the bear's rib cage to stimulate the heart. When much later the bear groggily sat up, Pierson boosted up its rear end and steered it around, wheelbarrow style, walking that bear in the woods most of the night until the drug wore off and the bear was able to navigate under its own power.

One clear sign that biologists really like their subjects is when they give them human names such as Big Mama, Little Sue, Mike, or Sister. Tim Burton, who has captured and released eighty-one bears while studying their food habits and population dynamics in northern California, pleads guilty to fondly naming the bears he has studied. One summer he captured a young female, Mary Ellen, nine times because she seemed to be addicted to the cheap strawberry jelly with which, along with cat food and marshmallows, he baited his culvert traps. Burton had to move his trap elsewhere because Mary Ellen was stacking his statistics.

In addition to Burton, many other bear research-

Above: *The drone of bees has attracted this young bear, and it is searching for the beehive—and the honey.*

Facing page: *It is June and this yearling brown bear may be on its own for the first time, abandoned by its mother, which will soon breed again.*

ers report that some black bears do deliberately enter traps time and again just to enjoy the food, despite the human handling that is certain to follow. A few even relax while biologists record their vital statistics. Burton points out that the same bears also keep returning to campgrounds, garbage dumps, and other places where food is available, and this is not in their best interests. Or in ours.

In Great Smoky Mountains National Park on the Tennessee–North Carolina border, panhandling bears threatened to become a greater problem than they were a pleasure to the millions of visitors who came to watch the bears every summer. Too many animals became hooked on the food that people illegally gave them, and this situation posed a real threat to the public safety. A few of the three hundred to five hundred

park bears became serious stalkers of camping areas. Some were so intelligent that they learned to distinguish the cars of park rangers from those of tourists. When a ranger drove up, the panhandling bruins would disappear into the woods until they left. The bears then returned to the roadside and the more generous tourists.

Gordon Burghardt and Michael Pelton are among many who have studied various aspects of black bear behavior in the Great Smokies. Using tape recorders, 35mm cameras, and video equipment in a remote enclosure, the two disproved an old belief that the species is colorblind, and instead verified that seeing color is an important way bears identify many natural foods. The men also learned the importance of ear positions, muzzle expressions, body postures, and vocalizations

A young bear in Glacier National Park watches a party of backpackers climbing a switchback on the trail below.

Sarsaparilla, Ben the Bear Hunter, and British Fur Hats

A few black bears have achieved fame; others have found themselves at the mercy of the infamous. One black bear, named Sarsaparilla, was widely known throughout Texas and the Southwest because it was the pet of the outlaw Judge Roy Bean, who held court at his Jersey Lily Saloon in Langtry, Texas. Because the bear had learned to swill beer from a bottle while sitting upright, Sarsaparilla attracted as great a following as the Jersey Lily herself—or the public hanging of a horse thief. The alcoholic animal was killed and skinned one day in a plot by San Antonio lawyer Bill Barnes, who held an old grudge against Judge Bean.

The hunter and frontiersman Ben Lilly became notorious for his almost religious crusade against grizzly bears in New Mexico during the late 1880s

and early 1890s. But before heading west, Lilly was a zealous black bear hunter, first in Louisiana and later in Texas where, single-handedly, he virtually eradicated all of the bears in the Big Thicket, a densely vegetated region of eastern Texas. Sadly, stories such as these are not unusual.

Much more recently Leo Del Villano, the mayor of Timmins, Ontario, read that the bearskin shakos, the tall fur hats worn by the guards at Buckingham Palace in London, were beginning to look moth-eaten. He wrote to the queen and offered to supply some three hundred fresh black bear hides to make new headgear. The British War Office in London replied that they would take as many as he could ship. Thus, in 1968 Del Villano organized "The Great Ontario Bear Hunt," as it was known.

Every weekend beginning in May of that year until June 15, teams of hunters from Timmins were dispatched guerrilla style, armed with every sort of legal weapon, to prowl the surrounding countryside and shoot every black bear they could find. They had to work fast before the bears, just out of hibernation, began to shed. The good news, depending on how you look at it, was that only sixty-two bears ever became hats, thanks to poor planning and execution. But the outcry from environmentalists, sports enthusiasts, and nature lovers in Canada, Great Britain, and the United States was so great that such hunts are unlikely to ever be repeated.

Above: *The black shako worn by a queen's guard in England might well have come from a black bear killed during the "Great Ontario Bear Hunt."* (Photo © Dick Dietrich)

Above: *The relatively long, thin snout rather than the black color indicate this is a black bear rather than a grizzly or brown bear.*

Facing page: *This bear may be licking the sap that drains from old claw marks as well as adding new claw scratches to the tree at the edge of its territory.*

when two animals meet or compete. They concluded that an approaching bear making any kind of sound is the one to carefully watch. It is not just being friendly. It is nervous, irritated, hungry, aggressive—or all of these.

THE BLACK AND THE GRIZZLY

Black bears share a good part of their more remote range, primarily in western Canada and Alaska, with grizzly bears, to which they are usually subordinate. For anyone traveling in this double-bear country it is very important to be able to distinguish one from the other, since grizzlies are potentially more dangerous. I should emphasize here that black bears deserve watching, despite the evidence in this chapter that

they are not really dangerous. But the potential is there, and I am always cautious when around them.

Size (grizzlies usually are larger) and color alone are not enough to tell black bears and grizzlies apart. Look instead for the pronounced hump on the grizzly's front shoulder, which black bears lack. Viewed from the side, blacks have longer, thinner snouts, while grizzlies have wider, more concave faces. There is also an almost undefinable difference in the way they walk. The typical grizzly seems to swagger a little more and appears more confident, which they usually are. Though it is not a good idea to approach black bears, coming in close contact with a grizzly is much more likely to be life-threatening. As we will see in the next chapter, the grizzly is a very different kind of bear.

Above: *This black bear is only weeks out of hibernation. Its coat is sleek and shiny, but by late summer it will shed and grow a new coat.*

Facing page: *Quaking aspen leaves in western North America are turning to gold, which is a signal to black bears. They must quickly add all the body fat they need to survive a winter in a den without food.*

Grizzly Bears

Snowplow crews had just finished scraping the last of winter's deep snow from the highways of Yellowstone National Park early one May morning when Peggy and I drove from our home in Jackson Hole, Wyoming, through the south entrance of the park at Flagg Ranch. In this area of Yellowstone, the road closely parallels the Snake River and provides a clear view of the waterway from the west bank. Immediately, we spotted two grizzly bears walking together downstream along the east bank of the Snake. They were not long out of hibernation. We judged the bears to be two-and-a-half-year-old siblings just beginning to explore their third springtime. Each weighed between 150 and 175 pounds (68–79 kg).

Suddenly, a coyote appeared from nowhere and, unbelievably, attacked the grizzlies head on. It snarled, snapped, lunged, and bit the bears in the face as if rabid, causing them to turn away and run up a steep bank away from the river. The coyote followed, attacking their rear ends until the bears were out of sight. At one point, one bear stopped and turned, snarling and striking at the other with foreclaws in a reaction biologists call displacement.

It was difficult to believe what we had witnessed: a coyote, weighing about thirty-five pounds (16 kg) at most, terrorizing two grizzly bears that together weighed as much as ten coyotes. But a few minutes later, we understood. The coyote returned to near the point of the original attack, and several small pups tumbled out of a well-hidden den to meet her. If not for that bold, nearly suicidal action, those cubs would have been a hot bear breakfast.

For a long time we pondered that remarkable encounter and wondered if the legendary ferocity of grizzly bears was really more fiction than fact. But a month later, from the trail to Mount Washburn's summit in Yellowstone, we located a small, female grizzly with twin cubs grazing on new green grass below a retreating

On a sunny, summer morning, a grizzly appears beside
Going-to-the-Sun Highway, Glacier National Park, and
briefly poses before crossing the road.

snowbank. As we watched through binoculars, a male grizzly appeared on the scene, also grazing, but moving directly toward the threesome. The moment she caught the scent of the boar, which was almost twice as large as she, the mother attacked head-on and sent the male racing away. The lesson is that, like people, all grizzlies are different. And they are unpredictable. Some run, some stand and fight, most avoid problems, while some even seem to look for trouble, depending on the situation and the bear's personality.

Native Americans who shared the grizzly bear's range in the western part of the continent lived in a kind of armed truce as equals with the bears. Many of the tribes acknowledged the great strength and intelligence of the grizzly, and even attributed magical powers to these fearsome mammals with long hair that was silvery in the low light of dawn and dusk. Bear cults and bear clans regarded grizzly bears as warrior ancestors, reincarnated. Sometimes the most brash young men in a clan, those with the most to prove, would hunt grizzlies with spears or bows and arrows, despite putting themselves in grave peril. A necklace of grizzly bear claws was considered powerful medicine and a symbol of bravery and leadership ability.

Early European explorers wandered widely over the American Southwest, which was grizzly country then, in the futile search for great golden cities. But those golden cities always turned out to be colorless adobe pueblos, and any bears encountered were shot out of fear and frustration, as well as for food. That was the beginning of the adversarial relationship between people and grizzlies—a relationship that continues, to some extent, today. Unlike the Native Americans who maintained an uneasy peace with bears, Europeans regarded *Ursus arctos horribilis* from the start as a dangerous obstacle and a threat to their "tam-

ing" of the North American wilderness.

The grizzly bear—*el oso, oso plateado,* silvertip, Ephraim, old Eph, Griz—is an impressive animal. Scientists agree that just one species, *Ursus arctos,* once occupied most of the land west of the Mississippi River from northern Mexico to the tip of the Alaskan Peninsula and the Arctic Coast. Due to a more abundant marine diet and probably some other factors, the coastal- and island-dwelling bears of Alaska on average are much larger than their inland cousins. These coastal bears are commonly known as brown, Peninsula, or Kodiak bears, the latter from Kodiak Island where they reach the greatest size of all. The Kodiak bears are classified as a separate subspecies, *Ursus arctos middendorfi,* while the other North American brown bears are classified with inland grizzlies as *Ursus arctos horribilis.* In this book we will discuss inland grizzlies and brown bears separately, because the two have very different personalities. They also live distinct lives in separate environments.

THE MIGHTY GRIZZLY

Even a very young bear of the subspecies *horribilis* can outperform the finest human athlete. It can run faster, swim better, endure greater punishment, and survive many times longer in frigid water. A grizzly has faster reflexes and is surely more agile. An adult grizzly can walk silently, stealthily pursuing prey. Until modern, high-velocity rifles came along, a grizzly's musculature and vascular system, as well as its very large heart and aorta, made it a difficult animal to subdue and almost impossible to kill before it caused a monstrous amount of damage.

A grizzly can reach nine hundred pounds (408 kg) when it is full-grown, healthy, and living in suitable habitat. But the average grizzly is closer to half that or less.

Still, at any weight the grizzly is a formidable creature. Skulls of elk, wolves, and even other bears have been fractured, spines and necks broken by a single blow from a grizzly's forepaw. Two powerful muscles

A male grizzly wanders over the colorful landscape of fall in Denali National Park, Alaska. It is fat and ready for the long, bitter winter not far off.

hinge its jaws and allow the animal to grind and shred almost any meal, even bone, that will fit in its mouth. Although not quite as dexterous with its arms and hands as a human, any grizzly can rotate its forearm well enough to use its long front claws like fingers for grasping and holding.

GRIZZLY POPULATION AND RANGE

When many Europeans still believed the world was flat, and Columbus finally proved otherwise, grizzlies lived throughout the western two-thirds of what is now the United States and across the western half of Canada, as well as in the northern Mexico states of Chihuahua and Coahuila. But nowhere in this huge area is the bear population more than a fraction of what it was in 1492, or even just a century ago.

In the mid-1990s, a consensus of government conservation agencies estimated the grizzly population south of the United States–Canada border to be about one thousand and hoped it was as high as fifteen hundred. Virtually all of these bears live in just three states: Montana, Wyoming, and Idaho. Most are concentrated in the Greater Yellowstone ecosystem, Glacier National Park, and the Bob Marshall Wilderness, south of Glacier; essentially they live in the central Rocky Mountains. But the species once roamed over the Great Plains, especially along large rivers, and in dry mountain ranges of the Southwest. They ranged northward throughout the Canadian tundra, almost to the Arctic saltwater shore and polar bear country. A few still cling to existence in that remote range, but their numbers are a tiny fraction of the former population. Peggy and I have seen grizzly bears there, along the bleak and lonely Dempster Highway, in the northern Yukon and just south of the remote Arctic settlement of Inuvik.

In 1991, a maverick grizzly bear wandered north far beyond the normal limits of the barren ground grizzly (*Ursus arctos ardsoni*), a rare subspecies living in the Arctic. It was found out on the frozen waters of Viscount Melville Sound between Banks, Melville, and Victoria Islands near 75 degrees north latitude, right in the midst of arctic Canada's polar bear country. Polar bear biologist Mitch Taylor estimated it was about ten years old and in the prime of life, certainly not a starving or displaced animal. When last seen, the wayward grizzly was plodding eastward across the ice-choked sea. Apparently, it had learned the polar bear technique of catching seals around breathing holes in the ice. This grizzly had also killed and eaten two polar bear cubs during its odyssey around the top of the earth.

Harder to believe today is that grizzlies once stalked the scenic coast of California and may even have been more abundant there five hundred years ago than anywhere else in their vast range. The Spanish explorer Sebastián Vizcaíno wrote about his landing in 1602 near modern-day Monterey. He found numerous bears feeding on a beached whale, and the bruins resented his intrusion. At least one of the grizzlies charged and drove the explorer away.

Grizzlies once grazed where Los Angeles and San Diego sprawl today. From Mexico to Washington State, Old Griz was the top of the food chain. More than two centuries after Vizcaíno, a southern California rancher wrote that bears were "like herds of swine, always hungry." When food was bountiful in a given area, grizzlies would gather by the hundreds, just as coastal brown bears gather along salmon streams today. But

California's Big Sur coastline is very much the same as two hundred years ago, except that the grizzlies which were once very numerous here are all gone. They are extinct in the Golden State.

The stunning scene from Swiftcurrent Lake, Glacier Park, conceals grizzly bears along with much other Rocky Mountain wildlife.

the silver-tipped bears and cattle ranching were not compatible, and Old Griz had to go. So the last of a species that thrived in California for thousands of years was shot in 1922 by a first-generation rancher. Now we have only a few mounted specimens gathering dust in museums, a few fading photographs, and the image on the state flag to remind us that grizzlies once owned the Golden State.

SENSES

Humans had their work cut out for them trying to exterminate the grizzlies, particularly the final, clever survivors, in California and elsewhere. The grizzlies that remain today are alert and wary creatures. Their sense of smell is extraordinary, at least as well developed as any of the other large, native mammals. They can locate carrion or sexual readiness in another bear from far away. Their hearing is at least adequate and may be quite good. But biologists and at least two photographers, namely Peggy and I, are undecided about the bear's vision.

Bears have spotted us from at least a quarter mile away, when the wind was blowing directly away from the bear toward us. But on one occasion when I stood out in the open behind a camera and tripod, an old female ambled toward me and walked right past, too close for my mental comfort or physical safety. But she continued on apparently without noticing me. Only when she was well behind me, where the breeze carried my scent, did this bear suddenly stop, turn around, and stand upright to see what she had missed. Bears stand up on hind legs for a better look around, not in preparation for an attack, as often has been written.

BEARS IN THE NIGHT

Grizzlies may be nocturnal, but perhaps not by choice. The majority and the most vicious of the bear-people incidents recorded in recent times have taken place at night. One theory suggests that grizzlies are naturally diurnal (creatures of the daylight hours), and they have become nocturnal primarily in areas frequented by people or where they feel hunting pressure. For example, the species tends to prowl around campsites and garbage dumps at night, while staying away during the day to avoid confrontations.

Most of the encounters between bears and members of the historic Lewis and Clark expeditions to the Pacific Coast in 1806 happened during the day. But these bears had seen very few people, all Native Americans with crude weapons, and the bears were not intimidated by any they met. It seems that bear habits have changed, and human society may have been the catalyst.

Today, grizzly bears act differently in the more remote, protected wilderness areas. The best place to see grizzly bears is in Denali National Park, Alaska. They have not been hunted there in several decades, and the bears are active throughout the long daylight hours of summer. They are out and about until the snows of September or early October close the park.

The evidence is strong that as more and more people invade the remaining grizzly bear country, the more the grizzly bears are evolving into a nocturnal species. And by all accounts, encounters with bears at night are more terrifying than in daylight.

A DIET OF PLANTS

Although an omnivorous species, most grizzlies consume far more vegetable matter than meat, especially

Above: *Kinnikinnick or bearberries, here growing in central Alaska, are a favorite food of many grizzlies.*

Facing page: *This large male grizzly was photographed dining on wild rose hips, eating the bushes and all.*

grasses, forbs, and roots. A single animal can eat a prodigious amount of low-growing berries during the summer and fall season. Watch a grizzly so engaged and you will see that a lot of berry bush disappears along with the berries. The earliest Americans learned a lot about which wild foods were edible and nutritious by noting what the bears ate.

In some years the nuts of the whitebark pine tree make up a good portion of the bears' diet; in other years bears don't eat whitebark pine nuts at all because few if any nuts are produced.

Penny Morgan, a professor at the University of Idaho, has been studying whitebark pine trees. During her research, she discovered, or rediscovered, how grizzlies are simply one part of the Yellowstone ecosystem, along with the pines; red squirrels; birds, such as Clark's nutcrackers; and even forest fires. Nutcrackers carry the seeds away from the trees and bury them for later use in winter. But they never find all that they have stored, and those that remain buried germinate. Under the right conditions the nuts become new trees. Every three to five years there is a bumper crop of nutritious nuts that fuel squirrels and bears alike. The best thing that can happen to a bear before heading toward hibernation in late fall is to find a large cache of high-fat seeds collected by squirrels. The bear will slowly burn this body fuel throughout the long, cold winter. Without the nutcrackers, the whitebarks would be unable to reproduce, and the grizzly bears would be denied this valuable energy source.

Dr. Morgan also found that without periodic fires from lightning storms, Engelmann spruce and subalpine firs replace the whitebarks, and these trees do not produce the seeds most valuable to the bears. Everything is connected in the natural world.

A DIET OF MEAT

Grizzlies eat meat as well as plant life. I have watched Wyoming grizzlies catching native cutthroat trout that spawn during springtime in shallow feeder brooks of Yellowstone Lake. Such fishing seems to be very hard work for the calories obtained. I have also watched bears digging for ground squirrels, and although they might catch a few, it also appears more energy is expended than gained.

A grizzly seems to be celebrating the warm and sunny morning by rolling in an alpine meadow. But it may also be trying to scratch loose the ticks imbedded in its back.

During the late spring in some parts of Alaska, grizzlies prey on newborn moose and caribou calves. Radio-telemetry studies in the Interior have shown that half of the moose calf mortalities that occur during the first six weeks of life are due to grizzlies. A few individual bears become efficient predators of adult moose. Wildlife photographer Johnny Johnson of Anchorage once observed a large bull caribou that had been harassed by wolves but escaped to a river bar where deep, swift river currents kept the wolves from following. But this was not a problem for a female grizzly, which waded to the island and within fifteen minutes had subdued the bull. The grizzly and her twin cubs fed on the bull for several days.

GRIZZLIES AND LIVESTOCK

According to some ranchers, grizzly bears prefer mutton and lamb chops to anything else. In September 1993, rancher Dave Grabbert of Emblem, Wyoming, claimed grizzlies killed at least five hundred of his sheep in the Shoshone National Forest, southeast of Yellowstone. That figure included, he said, one hundred animals that the bear had driven over a cliff. Grabbert further claimed that sheep ranchers in his area are helpless to protect their stock from grizzlies, because the bears are listed as a threatened species and cannot be shot. His claims made local headlines.

The Wyoming game managers who investigated the damage could find no proof that bears killed more than fifty sheep, if even that many. They pointed out that a sheepherder hired by Grabbert had abandoned the flock for a week, and that several electrical storms in the backcountry might also have taken a toll. They also believed some of the sheep Grabbert claimed were killed might still be alive and were grazing down already overgrazed areas. The state of Wyoming normally pays stock damage claims when game animals, bears, coyotes, mountain lions, or wolves are involved,

A grizzly cub, orphaned when a male killed its mother, survived for a time by eating nutritious soapberries in Denali National Park.

and the state negotiated a settlement with Grabbert. There always is local pressure to destroy alleged stock-killing bears, legally or illegally, even in areas where stock should not be allowed in the first place because the range is unsuitable or too fragile.

In May 1993, a family living near Lincoln, Montana, northwest of Helena, reported that a grizzly killed their pet pig and then returned to their property, perhaps looking for seconds. State wildlife officials trapped the bear and found that ear tags on the 375-pound (170-kg), four-year-old male matched those of a bear that had caused trouble before. Normally, a second major offense means the death penalty for such a problem bear. But just as the trapping crew tranquilized the animal, they heard a squeal, and the missing porker came trotting out of the woods, healthy and unscratched. It was a timely arrival. The bear was given a last minute reprieve and is now living a new life in Montana's Sun River Game Management Area, where he was released after being saved, strangely, by a pig.

EATING THEIR BRETHREN

Perhaps most surprisingly, grizzly bears will eat one another. In Alaska's Denali National Park in late May 1984, Peggy and I met biologist and University of Alaska professor Fred Dean and graduate student Laura Darling, who only days before had witnessed a fatal encounter between grizzly bears. A female and her twin yearling cubs were traveling near a bridge over the glacial Toklat River. At midday Dean saw a large, light-brown boar approach the trio. The boar and the mother huffed and growled at one another, and when the male rushed toward them, the terrified family scattered in different directions. The male pursued one yearling, a female, which it caught and struck with a forepaw, injuring the young bear. The mother tried to intervene, but the male brushed her aside and

again went after the yearling, which seemed paralyzed with fear. Again the female counterattacked, and for the next fifteen minutes the adults engaged in a terrible fight, sometimes rearing onto hind legs, until the female was thrown violently on her back. No longer able to move, she died, leaving two cubs, one seriously injured. The male fed on the female's carcass before covering it with earth and lying on top of it.

Park rangers shot the badly injured yearling, which weighed only about forty-five pounds (20 kg) and had no chance of recovering. The remaining cub, a male, lingered near his mother for more than two weeks. In fact, this orphaned cub was seen off and on for the next twelve weeks, never far from where the attack occurred. One afternoon we photographed him feeding on soapberries, and the cub seemed healthy. But it is doubtful that the cub could have fed sufficiently and managed the complex process of hibernating without the guidance of his mother.

Three weeks after the killing at Toklat Creek, and less than a half mile away, a large male, probably the same one, attacked another female with twin cubs. It captured and killed one of the cubs, but this mother did not resist. She and one cub escaped. Fred Dean told me he believed that males are responsible for the largest portion of the mortality among grizzly cubs.

There are also reports, not as well documented as these, of lone females killing and eating the cubs of others.

DIGGER, THE DAIRY QUEEN BEAR

One of my favorite grizzlies was one we never met, Number 22, nicknamed Digger by biologists Tim Thier and John Waller of Montana's Department of Fish, Wildlife, and Parks. Digger was a well-behaved traveler despite great temptations in the human world. Beginning in 1989 and continuing into 1994, Thier, Waller, and several co-workers conducted the South Fork (of the Flathead River) Grizzly Study to learn more about the bears in this area of northwestern Montana, a region that is critical to the species's survival. In addition to a thorough knowledge of bear biology and habits, as well as never-ending patience and determination, the study team members also needed cast-iron stomachs. The men began each day at dawn by loading rancid, maggoty, road-killed deer and other creatures into their pickups before heading for the mountains to bait or rebait traplines. The stench of the meat does indeed attract bears to traps, but it also draws flies and saturates vehicles, clothing—even clipboards. It can certainly ruin a person's appetite. To some, this live-trapping of large, mystical animals may seem glamorous, but the glitter is gone early each morning on

Bears and Bugs

Steve French is an emergency room physician at an Evanston, Wyoming, hospital, where his wife Marilyn is a nurse. The two are also very adventuresome, self-taught grizzly bear researchers and motion picture photographers who work mostly in Yellowstone National Park. One summer morning before daybreak, the two finished a hasty, cold breakfast and then began climbing into the high country above their wilderness camp. Well beyond the timberline above ten thousand feet (3,048 m) elevation, they came upon a surprising, if not incredible, sight. A "herd" of grizzly bears, eight in all, bunched fairly close together in a barren, glacial amphitheater.

This scene was hardly believable; grizzlies are natural loners. Except for the bond between sows and cubs, and for a brief fling during the breeding season when a male and female come together, grizzlies neither seek nor tolerate the company of others of their kind. Yet here the Frenches found eight gathered together.

At first, even through a high-powered spotting scope, the bears seemed to be licking rocks. Moving a little closer the pair realized that the huge animals were slurping up army cutworm moths. The herd had become remarkable in another way: grizzly bears were sharing a food source, which is almost unheard of behavior.

In time, the researchers would estimate that as many as one hundred different Yellowstone grizzlies spend at least part of their summers ingesting as many as ten thousand to twenty thousand of these insects each per day. From the eastern half of the country and the Great Plains, these moths migrate to the Rocky Mountains in summer, where they feed on the nectar of alpine wildflowers at night and cluster among the rocks during the day. Composed of about 70 percent fat and 30 percent protein, the moths provide relatively more nutrition and energy than a deer fawn, an elk calf, a cutthroat trout, or a ground squirrel. No wonder the bears look for moth swarming areas and live well on them as long as the supply lasts. As the Frenches saw in that mountain meadow, grizzlies are even willing to forego instinct and tolerate each other in order to gorge on the moths.

the job.

One of the forty-eight grizzlies trapped, weighed, examined, recorded, radio-collared, and released was Digger. On being snared, most bears go into a rage, trying to dig their way to freedom while tearing up everything they can reach with claws and teeth, until they are tranquilized. A few play possum. They crouch, motionless, and then lunge at the last minute toward approaching biologists. Digger also remained still, but he didn't lunge. The young bear remained fairly docile while the biologist put him to sleep and fitted him with a permanent collar.

Since his capture, Digger has wandered over a very wide range, always tracked by radio, from near the resort town of Bigfork on Flathead Lake, thirty miles (48 km) north to near Columbia Falls. He climbed twenty miles (32 km) over a high divide, through deep snowdrifts into the Middle Fork of the Flathead River—and back again. Somehow, unerringly, he found his way to where a series of train derailments in 1989–90 on the Burlington Northern line spilled 125 tons (114 tonnes) of corn near Bear Creek and Glacier Park's southern boundary. In the summer of 1990, Digger was one of several bears observed eating and fattening up on the fermenting grain. As many as fifteen to twenty bears could be sighted there at one time. Nine were killed by passing freight trains and cars, but Digger avoided the danger and eventually left the accident scene, only to find a road-killed elk carcass nearby. The feast continued, as he ate all of it.

Digger did not go into hibernation until mid-December, much later than is normal in this region. In fact, he was a habitually late hibernator, even using the same overwinter den twice.

Above: *In the northern Rocky Mountains, the Columbian ground squirrel is a source of protein for many grizzlies. Considerable digging may be required.*

Left: *A grizzly wandering over foothills of the Alaska Range might well meet a bull caribou such as this grazing on the same plants.*

Maybe the most remarkable aspect of Digger's life is that he spent most of it very close to people, usually without anyone but the radio-trackers realizing it, and without ever getting into trouble. He simply stayed out of sight of humans. Late in 1992 Digger was tracked within two hundred yards (183 m) of the Dairy Queen restaurant in Bigfork, seldom being spotted. Despite the obvious temptation and rich odors emanating from a place like this, Digger still stayed out of trouble.

Digger also loved to hang around the numerous apple orchards when the fruit ripened in the Flathead Valley. He was especially fond of visiting the orchards of brothers Art and Jack Whitney, eighty-one and seventy-six years old respectively, and Digger remained around their place, not far from the heart of Bigfork, for several weeks. Maybe the bear felt more welcome here than elsewhere. Both men were conservationists; Jack was one of the state's top bowhunters;

and even though Digger broke down a few old apple trees in his zeal, he was only "behaving naturally." One day Jack Whitney caught Digger watching him intently from about forty feet away (12 m), but he said he felt no fear of the now familiar animal. "Bears," Whitney said, "had first claim to the land." He missed Digger, he admitted, when eventually the bear wandered away.

Not all of the Whitneys' neighbors were as enchanted with the newly named Dairy Queen Bear. Mrs. Jim Lefever, who operates Rosie's Hair Corral in her home, became afraid to work in her flower garden where she found bear tracks. In fact, she did not walk outside much at all after that. Digger did raid the Lefever's garbage can one night, spewing the discarded contents over a wide area, as sort of a parting shot at unsociable folks, before finally clearing out. It is possible we will hear more about this remarkable animal in the future.

GRIZZLIES AND PEOPLE

Human-bear incidents often occur when a person comes between a sow and her cubs or approaches a family group too closely. There are many records of females protecting cubs with blind rage, from other bears and wolves as well as people. But, unpredictably, other grizzly mothers will run rather than fight. Backcountry outfitter Gene Wade of Cooke City, Montana, told me of once accidentally leading his string of pack horses on a steep mountain trail and then suddenly realizing that he and his horses had separated a mother from twin cubs. He expected an attack, but this female turned and ran over the next ridge without once looking back. The cubs followed, but for at least two hundred yards (183 m) they never saw anything except mama's rear end. Though such behavior is not unusual, it cannot be counted on.

Val "Blackie" Blackburn also had a frightening experience with a grizzly bear. A professional fur trapper in Alaska's Lake Minchumina area, northwest of Denali National Park, Blackburn had been away from his Six Mile Cabin for several weeks and was returning by dog team to spend Thanksgiving and Christmas at home. The cabin was halfway, and he planned to overnight there. His sled was loaded with pine marten and lynx pelts, a sleeping bag, a rifle, and the last of Blackburn's grub. Nearing the cabin, he sensed trouble. There were fresh grizzly tracks in the snow everywhere, which was strange, because grizzlies should have been in hibernation for at least a month. However, the temperature was a little "warm" at 20 degrees Fahrenheit (-6° C).

Suddenly, a grizzly materialized between Blackburn and his cabin. He pulled the rifle from his sled, shot too rapidly, and wounded the bear. It flinched, turned, and came after the trapper again, but a second shot stopped the grizzly. Walking somewhat weak-kneed into the cabin, the trapper realized the bear had been sleeping inside and may even have been slowly starving to death. There was no food left on the shelves. On skinning the bear, Blackburn found it was thin and in no condition to begin hibernating, though it was a very big animal. Blackburn almost discarded the skull but, thinking twice, he measured it. By the Boone and Crockett system it scored twenty-six inches and remains today among the largest grizzlies taken in inland Alaska, or anywhere.

Despite Blackburn's experience, relatively few grizzly bears suffer from starvation. Some seem to develop a craving for good old country cooking, like a certain young 170-pound (77-kg) male in Yellowstone National Park.

Every summer evening there is a barbecue cook-out for guests of the Roosevelt Lodge near Tower Junction in the northern portion of the park. One fine evening in August 1990, this young bear suddenly crashed the party and tried to gobble up as much of the food laid out for 180 diners as he could stuff into his stomach. The guests graciously vacated the area, as did the bear when he had eaten his fill.

The history of this cub, one of an estimated 200 to 220 grizzlies living in Yellowstone in 1994, is interesting and revealing. His mother, tagged Number 134, had been trapped several times as a nuisance bear in the park's Fishing Bridge area. After the most recent incident, she was deemed incorrigible and was banished to a research lab at Washington State University. Apparently her cub had learned some bad habits from his mother; the cub also was live-trapped (after the barbecue episode) and was moved to a distant area of the park. Exile seemed to have the desired effect on the cub, as nothing more was heard from him that

A Moose, a Bear, and a Cessna

Alaskan Ed Gurtner, a hunter, left five hundred pounds (227 kg) of fresh moose meat in his Cessna 170 bush plane, which was tied down near Cripple Creek in the central part of the state. When he returned to the craft, a grizzly was inside tearing it apart trying to get at the meat. Gurtner fired a shot, but the bear was not intimidated. Now irritated by the gunfire as well as hungry, the grizzly got under the plane, picked up the fuselage, and slammed it down. The bear then turned toward Gurtner, and the pilot had to make his getaway in a boat beached nearby. The next morning about three hundred pounds of meat was missing, and the plane damage was estimated at fifteen thousand dollars.

The bear that destroyed the airplane undoubtedly had similar brawn to this large, dominant male.

summer. He probably began his first hibernation alone in late October.

GRIZZLIES KILLING PEOPLE

Late on an August afternoon in 1967, teenage backpackers Roy Ducat and Julie Helgeson hit the rocky trail along the Garden Wall in Montana's spectacular Glacier National Park. Both were summer park employees with a day off from work. They headed from Logan Pass into the high country toward Granite Park Chalet, an old backcountry hostel. Ducat and Helgeson knew there were bears in the area—in fact bears ranged throughout the park—and they also knew the grizzlies rarely confronted humans. At dusk, the two unrolled sleeping bags in a designated campsite, which was already occupied by three other backpackers, 450 yards (410 m) from the chalet. After chatting in the dark until about 9:30, they zipped up their bags and fell asleep. The next thing Ducat remembers is hearing shuffling noises and Helgeson saying, "Bear. Don't move."

Seconds later Ducat felt a bear bite deeply into his shoulder, and he was pulled from his bag and yanked into the air. Ducat tried to play dead and not scream despite dangling from the mouth of a grizzly. The bear dropped him, turned to Helgeson, and grabbed her in its jaws. Although she screamed loudly enough that someone was awakened at the chalet, the animal dragged her away down a steep slope. The badly injured Ducat could do nothing, and he went into shock. However, he survived.

A rescue party quickly organized at the chalet and, with flashlights and a rifle, they followed the bloody trail. Only one hundred yards (91 m) from the campsite, they found the badly mauled young woman and carried her to the chalet, where she later died of her injuries.

Horrible as this incident was, it was not all that happened on that fateful night. Only nine and a half miles (15 km) away, another grizzly bear attacked five park employees camping in the Trout Lake area of Glacier, a popular fishing destination. These campers, like Ducat and Helgeson, were aware of grizzly activity in the area. Early that evening, an unusually scrawny female bear had chased the group into the lake and had eaten their food. It also carried away Michele Koons's pack.

The five were terrified, but they decided it would be more dangerous to pack out in the pitch dark than to stay until morning. No one slept at all, and they built a roaring campfire, which they kept constantly fueled. From time to time, they could hear a bear

prowling around their campsite beyond the firelight. At about 4:30 A.M., the grizzly suddenly charged in among the campers and bit Paul Dunn. Four of the campers jumped out of their bags, but Koons was trapped inside by a stuck zipper. The animal grabbed her and her screams were the last sounds she made.

The reason or reasons for these two rare and almost identical tragedies to happen at about the same time that night remain unknown. The grizzly bears of Glacier National Park have always been, or seemed to be, more dangerous than *Ursus arctos horribilis* elsewhere. In recent times, we have heard of bear attacks and casualties in Glacier far more frequently than from anywhere else. All incidents, whether in Glacier or in other parts of the grizzly's range, are faithfully reported, because bear attacks make bigger headlines than auto accidents, falls, drowning, climbing deaths, and most homicides, even though such events cause many times the number of fatalities. Still, that horrible night seemed, and still seems, terrifying beyond words. In a sense, it may have been a tragedy almost a century in the making, and the dual deaths began a debate that continues today.

This much is certain. Almost every year, a few humans are killed by grizzly bears in North America. Nine fatalities were reported in 1995, and this was slightly higher than in recent seasons. While a person traveling in bear country should keep this always in mind—and be careful—bears are far from a major cause of backcountry deaths anywhere.

CAN HUMANS AND BEARS COEXIST IN NATIONAL PARKS?

Gairdner B. Moment, a scientist writing in *Bioscience* magazine after the Glacier attacks, believed we must make up our minds whether to run parks for bears or for people. If parks are for people, Moment suggested, then we must try to conserve the bear on other lands. But most biologists strongly believe in accommodating both humans and bears. They believe bears and people can coexist in the parks, but realize that better regulation is needed.

Quills in its nose are evidence that this young Alaskan grizzly has just had an encounter with a porcupine—and lost.

Adult grizzlies pause in a warm pool in Yellowstone Park and spar briefly before disappearing into the forest. It is June and this may be a mating pair.

For starters, we need to continue to firmly address the old problem of allowing grizzlies access to human food. When problems between humans and bears arise, they are almost always about food. As recently as the 1940s, bears were allowed to eat at feeding stations near Old Faithful in Yellowstone, dining on the garbage from the park hotel dining rooms, which was provided while tourists watched from behind fences. The illegal feeding of bears had also taken place around Granite Chalet and at Trout Lake up until the fateful night that Julie Helgeson and Michele Koons were killed. Today, such illegal feeding almost certainly has stopped.

Frank and John Craighead conducted a seven-year study of grizzly bears in Yellowstone Park from 1959 to 1966. This landmark study is the basis for much of the scientific knowledge we have about the grizzly today. Not long ago, Frank and I discussed the grizzly in the national parks. "Grizzlies are wilderness animals," says Craighead, "and most remain in wilder-

ness unless lured out by easily available food. They must never be fed, or allowed to feed in areas frequented by people. National parks certainly can and should be both for bears and people."

The late, irreverent, environmental writer Edward Abbey looked at grizzly bears in still another way. "They're necessary," he wrote. "If there's nothing bigger and meaner than you out there, it's not really wilderness." Another old friend, Montana outfitter Gene Wade, agrees: "There are two kinds of country out there: with and without grizzly bears. Being out in one is tame, the other is high adventure."

THE CRAIGHEAD STUDY

High adventure is exactly what describes the life of the Craighead brothers even before their famous grizzly study. The sons of a naturalist, they roped down into canyons to study falcon eyries and shot through whitewater rapids in a raft early in life. During the Craigheads' service in the U.S. Navy during World War

Above: *What appears to be a threat or aggression here is really a grizzly yawning on a hot summer day. Sometimes yawning can be a sign of irritation or unease.*

Overleaf: *It is early spring in Denali and the grizzly has just emerged from winter's hibernation. Its priority now is to find food—new green vegetation or a winter-killed carcass.*

II, the military abandoned the twins on a Pacific atoll to test jungle equipment and survival theories. That wilderness experience led to their decision to study natural history when the war ended. Once out of the service, the brothers obtained funding from the National Geographic Society, the National Science Foundation, and other sources to begin their now well-known Yellowstone grizzly research. The Craigheads were pioneers in the use of bio-telemetry to gather information. For the first time, scientists could follow the movements of animals in areas physically inaccessible to humans, such as through thick forests, over mountain passes, and into dens.

Even so, it wasn't easy work because the bears first had to be trapped, anesthetized, and color-tagged for identification. Reading about this in Frank's exciting book, *Track of the Grizzly*, is almost like reading science fiction, except that this is gospel truth. In the book, Frank describes the many fascinating bears he encountered. There was Cutlip, with a lower lip torn

in a long-ago fight; Loverboy, scarred over one eye and missing part of an ear; G.I., named because she strictly disciplined her cubs; Owl Face, which reminded Frank of a short-eared owl; the Sucostrin Kid, which needed more than a normal dose of the drug sucostrin for tranquilization; Marian, described in the sidebar on page 80; and numerous others.

From the many bears the Craigheads had under electronic scrutiny, the brothers gained great respect for a magnificent animal. They realized that the keys to grizzly life are living space, size, aggressiveness, and experience. Unless he is past his prime, the largest and oldest male is the king of the hill, the dominant bear. Both sexes are promiscuous and need vast territory to roam. One to four cubs are born in winter dens selected well before hibernation, and the mothers exclusively dig out the den from scratch or expand an existing cavity. In the Craighead study, the bears tended to reuse the same hibernation sites, which is unusual and not common elsewhere. The average litter size is two, and male cubs outnumber female cubs two to one. Half of all cubs do not survive beyond their first one and a half years. By the time they are three or four years old, there are as many females as males. Overall, the Craighead study counted more females than males in the adult population.

The average lifespan of the grizzlies in Yellowstone was only five to six years. Hunting was then legal outside park boundaries, and because many bears wandered outside Yellowstone, about 40 percent were shot. A few very reclusive or tenacious bears lived to be twenty-five years old, and some may have survived even longer. Bears died from old age, disease, accidents, or fighting, all causes that are difficult to confirm, even with telemetry. Some simply disappeared.

The dens investigated by the Craigheads and their assistant Maurice Hornocker, who would later become well-known for his studies of mountain lions and Siberian tigers, always seemed carefully chosen and warm. Some were on slopes or in canyon walls, which were difficult to access and subject to avalanches. All were on slopes facing north, so that the snow sealing the entrances did not thaw during brief, unseasonable warm spells. The dens were lined and insulated with fir and pine boughs, which the animals raked and carried inside in their mouths. Expectant mothers seemed to prepare softer, deeper bough beds than boars and other females. They may have slept right through the birth of the cubs in December or January. All of the Yellowstone bears go into hibernation at almost exactly the same time.

As with black bears, it is likely that grizzly bears reach their maximum age in sanctuaries such as Yellowstone where hunting is not a factor. But then there is an Alaskan bear to be considered. In the fall of 1982, Donna Lipan of Staten Island, New York, was hunting with outfitter Phil Driver along the east slope of Alaska's Brooks Range north of Kotzebue, near the northern limit of grizzly range, when she shot a grizzly that apparently had seen better days. Its hair was long and sleek, but there was little fat on the body, and its teeth were very well worn. From those teeth, Alaska Department of Fish and Game biologists determined that the animal was between thirty-two and thirty-three years old. It might be the oldest wild bear on record.

OUTLAW GRIZZLIES OF THE OLD WEST

The historical accounts of the nineteenth-century American West are rife with tales of bears that be-

Above: *The claws of an adult grizzly are long and sharp, useful in defense and for stripping berries from bushes.*

Facing page: *This young grizzly is not long out of hibernation and on its own after spending 2½ years with its mother. From this time onward, survival will be tougher.*

Marian, the Pioneer Bear

The first bear captured, officially designated Number 40 but unofficially nicknamed Marian, became an important part of the Craighead study. The Craigheads trapped her on July 1, 1960, when she was two and a half years old and weighed 175 pounds (79 kg). They tagged the bear and then set her free. A year later the gate of the Craighead's culvert trap clanged shut again, with Marian once more inside. She now weighed 300

For a long time, Marian wandered freely throughout Yellowstone, always under the surveillance of the Craighead brothers.

pounds (136 kg). Before releasing her a second time, the Craigheads fitted Marian with a new type of collar containing a radio transmitter. The collar weighed about two pounds (0.9 kg), was waterproofed in silicone material, and was hoped to be shockproof and bear-proof as well. With the collar in place, the first such on a grizzly anywhere in the world and the first of twenty-nine grizzlies to date so instrumented in Yellowstone, Marian walked away into a late summer snowstorm, monitored as no bear had ever been before. The brothers wondered if they would ever see Marian again. Fortunately they did, on a remote mountainside, inadvertently almost stumbling over the female bear as she slept in her day bed. Many bears would charge anyone who surprised them like this, but Marian did not. She ran away. During the next eight years, Marian, within her thirty-square-mile (78-sq-km) range, traveled, foraged, met other grizzlies, mated, raised cubs, and generally avoided people she saw from afar. In late fall 1968, the sow curled up in a den she herself had dug, with three sleepy cubs beside her.

After furnishing vital bear data for almost nine years, Marian was shot on the morning of October 13, 1969. That summer there was a critical shortage of both wild berries and whitebark pine nuts, so Marian began to forage in the vicinity of Lake Hotel, where the scent of human food was in the air. Near the hotel she charged a ranger who was trying to immobilize one of her cubs caught in a trap, and Marian, sadly, paid for it with her life.

Marian's three cubs were released and they survived for a short while on their own. One wandered to the far southern region of the park near Flagg Ranch, where it was killed by a poacher not far from where Peggy and I later saw the mother coyote attack the grizzly cubs. Another was shot legally near the town of West Yellowstone, Montana, outside the national park. The third disappeared in 1972.

came rogues. These "outlaw" grizzlies and cattle killers often had colorful names such as Old Mose, Blueface, Bloody Paws, Red Robber, Bandit, Old Silver, and Two Toes.

Two Toes was one of the best known, most notorious of the outlaw grizzlies. Even school boys across America read about this remarkable animal in paperbacks and newspapers of the era. His career began in the spring of 1902, when Caleb Myres, a hired hand, led a trail drive north through Montana's Swan Valley, south of what was soon to become Glacier National Park. Barely underway, Myres was given command when his boss and chief wrangler were killed in a gunfight. More trouble followed. The drive got a late start, and many of the cows were calving now and trailing the herd. A grizzly bear started following the cows and killing the stragglers. Tracks left behind by the bear revealed that two toes and half of a forepaw were missing—the calling card of Two Toes.

Some years earlier Two Toes had walked into a trap baited with a dead mule deer and chained to a tree, deliberately set for him. He dragged the trap, tree and all, for almost a mile before tearing and chewing his paw free of the iron jaws. Two Toes also snapped off several teeth while trying to free himself, which might well have exposed raw nerves. The experience probably explains why Two Toes never stepped in another of the hundreds of traps set for him.

Two Toes killed and ate cattle whenever he was hungry—and that seemed to be all the time. He demolished a chuckwagon while the crew was working a roundup. He killed three horses that belonged to a hunting party of Blackfoot Indians. Bounty hunters arrived on the scene, hoping to cash in on the many bounties offered for the hide of the outlaw bear. A veteran hunter and trapper named Kline was hired to kill the bear.

Kline followed Two Toes for three months before even catching a glimpse of the bear. Kline then made a hasty shot at the running target and wounded the grizzly. Two Toes bawled horribly before disappearing into the timber. The painful cries were followed by silence.

Kline began to follow a trail of dark blood drops, perhaps too confidently. The blood led into heavy brush, where Two Toes caught the bounty hunter with a forearm blow under the armpit that sent him airborne. Kline later woke up in the dark. He was cold, in great pain, and unable to stand up. He would have died on the spot, had a prospector not found him the next morning. Badly mauled and in deep shock, Kline was carried on horseback to a hospital in Missoula. He survived, but limped badly and never fully recovered his health.

Before statehood in 1889, the reward for shooting a human cattle rustler in Montana territory had been two hundred dollars. In 1902, that same figure was offered for Two Toes, although no one in Swan Valley thought a penny would ever have to be paid for the elusive, legendary grizzly. Around the same time, the cattle killing suddenly stopped, and some ranchers concluded that Kline had indeed fatally wounded Two Toes, as he claimed.

But two years later in the spring of 1904, trouble began all over again. Twenty-nine calves were found dead, along with a few steers and cows. The unmistakable footprint calling cards were left behind. Two Toes sometimes seemed in too big a hurry to eat his kills, leaving them for wolves and coyotes to finish. Over time the bear ranged over one thousand square miles (2,600 sq km), appearing and disappearing like a ghost, seeming to taunt ranchers. Two Toes nearly tore the head from the body of a favorite horse that Caleb Myres had tethered to a tree while investigating a heifer mangled by . . . Two Toes.

The depredations went on through 1905, a year when ranchers were preoccupied with human outlaws who were rustling cattle by driving entire herds north into Canada. Winter arrived early that year, with a heavy snowfall in September, and the attacks stopped. But in the spring of 1906, Two Toes again went on a rampage. In desperation the local stockmen's association hired Henri Belieu, a well-known big game hunter and trapper. For killing Two Toes he was guaranteed $675, a figure that would compare to about $20,000 today.

Belieu wasted no time. With two vicious Airedales and a stroke of luck, he soon located Two Toes. The Airedales attacked the bear, which immediately snapped the back of one dog and almost split the other in half before Belieu could intervene. Losing his canine friends so enraged the Frenchman that he swore

to kill Two Toes for revenge and honor alone. Belieu never slacked his efforts and shot three innocent grizzlies and several black bears while pursuing Two Toes. But he never again saw his quarry. After finding Two Toe's tracks behind him, however, he started watching his back trail a lot more carefully.

Late in the fall of 1906, two eastern hunters hired Missoula outfitters George Murphy and a man known only as Dale to guide them on a hunt for trophy bighorn sheep and elk. One day as they were packing between high hunting camps, their string of horses came nervously to a cul-de-sac, without space to continue on or turn around. Searching for a way out, Dale happened to look up and stared into the face of a huge grizzly bear. The horses panicked and tried to throw off their packs, as the bear clicked his teeth and came full bore down the slope toward the trapped pack train. Somehow Dale managed to stay calm, slip out of his saddle with his brand new .45/90 rifle, and begin firing.

One shot caught Two Toes in the neck, another through the ribs and into the lungs. A third ricocheted

Above: *An adult scratches its back on the roadsign that reads "Sable Pass," which is an important grizzly bear viewing area in Denali National Park.*

Left: *Typical grizzly bear country in Denali National Park. Traveling bears, especially males, follow the course of the Toklat and other glacial rivers here.*

off the bear's skull, behind the left ear. Dale's body shook uncontrollably as he watched the bear's lifeblood drain from its mouth. Thus, Dale, not Belieu, collected the Two Toes reward. Nobody knows what happened to Dale after he killed the legendary bear. He may well have given up guiding forever.

Two Toes was estimated to weigh about 1,100 pounds (500 kg). He may have been as old as fifteen, and he was fat and in good physical condition, although he was badly scarred around the face. And of course he had the mangled forepaw. After a four-year

reign of killing, which included an estimated $100,000 worth of livestock (in 1995 figures), Two Toes was converted into an open-mouthed rug, present location unknown.

THE END OF THE GRIZZLY IN THE SOUTHWEST

Just as a few grizzly bears accomplished a good bit of damage to livestock herds that invaded the bear's original range in the North American West, a few specialized human hunters killed a disproportionate number of bears. In the Southwest, the demise of the

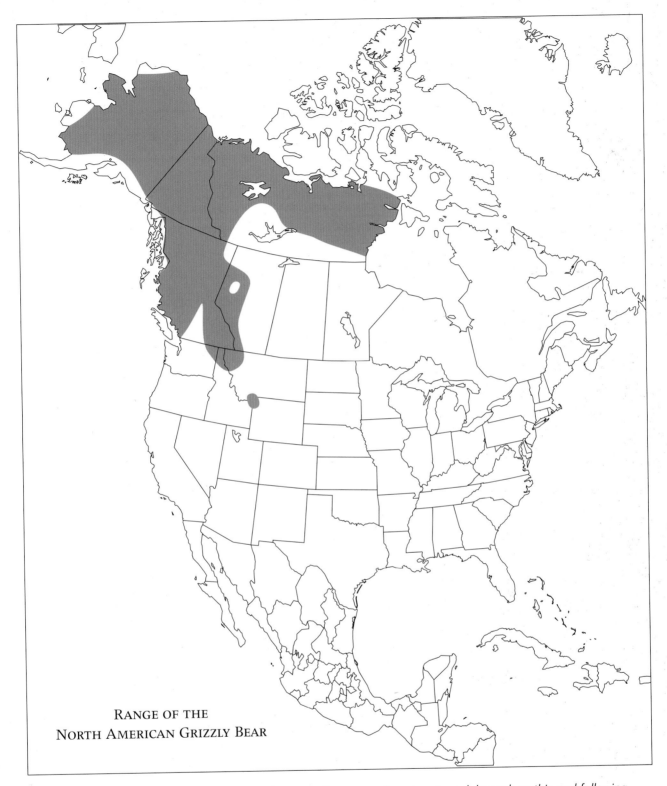

RANGE OF THE
NORTH AMERICAN GRIZZLY BEAR

Facing page: *Much of what we know today about grizzlies comes from tagging adults such as this and following their movements through radio telemetry.*

grizzlies can be traced to a few men who virtually devoted their lives to the task. Most were unsociable, single-minded, but skilled woodsmen, who were also self-sufficient survivalists and usually good horsemen. They had no trace of a conservation ethic and seemed consumed by the process of bringing wild animals, bears especially, to what they considered justice. They were avenging angels with long beards and cold eyes. In their determination to destroy the wild creatures

that lured the hunters into the wilderness in the first place, many of these legendary old bear hunters were in fact laying waste to their own way of life.

Ben Lilly was the archetype of the early 1900s grizzly hunter. As I wrote in the black bear chapter, Lilly took a terrible toll on that species in Texas and Louisiana before he "escaped" from farming, the restrictions of society, and a nagging wife and family, first to northern Mexico and then to New Mexico.

A grizzly naps on Alaskan tundra changing to bright fall colors. The bear may also be watching a colony of Arctic ground squirrels nearby.

Many who knew him best said that Ben Lilly was a lot like the predators he hunted. Lilly was known to eat tremendous amounts of meat when he had it, and then go days without anything. He did not drink alcohol, smoke, or chase women. He slept outdoors, without regard to the weather, winter or summer. His camp gear consisted of a tin cup, a tin can, and sometimes a skillet. He killed dogs that did not prove worthy as lion or bear hunters.

For a while Lilly worked for the newly organized Predator and Rodent Control Branch of the old U.S. Biological Survey (forerunner of the U.S. Fish and Wildlife Service), a bureau that spent millions of dollars over many years killing huge numbers of wild animals for no sensible reason. Lilly was hired to guide multimillionaire railroad magnates, as well as President Theodore Roosevelt. But these hunts seldom worked out very well, because Lilly was by nature a loner who hunted best by himself. He was highly unsuited to helping others. After thirty years or so of roaming the West, Lilly left behind a trail of dead grizzly bears, as well as black bears, cougars, and wolves; nobody will ever know the exact terrible toll. But when Lilly died in 1936, just short of eighty years old, very few grizzlies remained alive in New Mexico or in the entire Southwest. The last grizzly in Arizona had been killed the year before. The last one in Mexico was shot in 1960 in the Sierra del Nido in the northern state of Coahuila.

Officials in Colorado have considered grizzlies extinct in that state since at least the early 1960s, and for many years no evidence surfaced to the contrary. But a strange event occurred in September 1979 which seemed to cast doubt on the official position.

Outfitter Ed Wiseman was guiding Kansas archer Mike Niederee on a hunt for elk in the San Juan Mountains. According to Niederee's testimony later, they inadvertently came upon a sleeping bear. It jumped up and ran directly at Wiseman, knocking him down and biting him. Wiseman tried to lie still, hoping it would go away, but the bear kept mauling him. Wiseman managed to reach a hunting arrow on the ground nearby and began stabbing the mauler in the throat. Weakened, the bear released Wiseman, walked a short distance away, and died. This account was not accepted by everyone in the region.

Wiseman might also have perished, but Niederee had training in first aid, and he treated Wiseman before leaving to get horses and help. A rescue team

A female in almost human posture, enjoying a hot pool bath in Yellowstone.

reached Wiseman and brought him out of the wilderness alive. The bear carcass also was retrieved and, astonishingly, it was determined to be a grizzly, the first seen in Colorado in more than a quarter of a century. The bear was a female more than sixteen years old, between 350 and 400 pounds (159–181 kg) and in very good condition. Its reproductive history could not be determined because the uterus had spoiled before it could be examined. This probably was the last grizzly living wild in the Southwest and almost certainly had been alone for many years. Several surveys in the San Juan Mountains since 1979 have turned up no other conclusive signs of *Ursus arctos horribilis*.

Maybe, just maybe there could be others. A few diehards, like those that hunt sunken treasures at sea, are still looking.

A mother disciplines a surprised cub that has been wandering too far away. Wandering too far from mother is dangerous if there is a male bear in the vicinity. Males kill, sometimes eat, any small cubs they can catch.

Facing page: A grizzly cub swings at a bee that has been hovering around its face.

Above: *A single grizzly used this den at least one winter northeast of Yellowstone Park. It is located on the north slope of a mountain at about 7,000 feet elevation.*

Right: *The future of this and all other grizzlies depends on our saving intact sufficient wilderness areas in western North America.*

Brown Bears

O n a typical cool, gray morning along Alaska's magnificent southwestern coast, Peggy and I, aboard the M.V. Waters, are anchored in sheltered Hallo Bay just offshore. Through binoculars I have spotted a large brown bear on the beach. The animal is digging for clams head-down near the water's edge, and only its rump is visible. As we watch, a dense bank of fog from the Bering Sea rolls in, smothering Shelikof Strait and obliterating our view.

Mike Parks, the skipper of our boat, joins us on deck. He has been listening to a radio weather report. "It might," Mike says without conviction, "clear up soon and we can go ashore."

This is not the most encouraging news for photographers on assignment to shoot Alaskan brown bears. If anything in coastal Alaska is more unpredictable than bears, it is the weather; it can be foul for long periods of time. An hour or so and many cups of coffee later, a fresh wind begins to blow, exposing first the snow-capped mountains of Katmai National Park and then, finally, the shore.

The bear is still digging away like a huge gopher. While Mike lowers an outboard skiff to the water, Peggy and I pull on waders and collect our cameras, lenses, tripods, and backpacks. Polly Hessing, an experienced bear biologist who is also our guide, joins us in the boat, toting a twelve-gauge shotgun. Mike starts the damp, reluctant outboard motor and aims the boat toward the wilderness shore.

From the first cough of the outboard, the bear we've been watching stops clamming and watches us. As we approach the beach, we realize that the bear is no longer alone. Farther inland, two more brown bears, standing belly-deep in a shallow tidal stream, are studying us intently. Our boat scrapes gravel, and we nervously prepare to step out onto solid ground. Polly goes first, and we gather our gear from the skiff and follow her, always moving slowly and deliberately. My pulse pounds as I extend

A young brown bear stands erect in a shallow stream to
better spot incoming schools of spawning salmon.
Katmai, Alaska.

tripod legs into the sand and attach a 600mm lens to my camera.

As I look into my viewfinder, the scene around us comes to life. The clam-digging bear is running away from us as fast as a six-hundred- or seven-hundred-pound (272–318-kg) mammal can travel. This is good news in terms of safety, but the rapidly shrinking back end of a brown bear is not an ideal photographic portrait. However, the other two bears are tromping through a stream, running directly *toward* us at a good clip. I wonder what exactly I am doing in their path, especially when I see Mike make a move back toward the beached boat. But Polly stands fast. Then, as abruptly as they started, the bears stop and pounce back into the middle of the stream. Water splashes everywhere, and one of the bears emerges from the spray with a salmon in its jaws. Bright-red roe squirts into the air, and the bear squats down to

our time on that beach do any of the animals seem to notice us. It is the beginning of a fine brown bear adventure.

THE MIGHTY BROWN BEAR

These coastal brown bears, which are also called marine, Kodiak, or Peninsula bears, are of the same genus and species, *Ursus arctos*, as the inland grizzly bears discussed in the previous chapter. But in living where they do, close to saltwater where larger quantities of richer food are easily available, the bears have an advantage over the grizzlies. The food base of such sanctuaries as Katmai, McNeil, and the vicinity can support forty times the density of bears—the biomass—as can much larger Denali National Park in Alaska's interior. Brown bears are also larger and seem somehow different from their inland cousins. However, only the brown bears on and around Kodiak Island are classified as a separate subspecies, *Ursus arctos Middendorfi*. The other North American brown bears are grouped with the inland grizzlies under *Ursus arctos horribilis*.

Anatomically, brown bears are almost indistinguishable from inland grizzlies, but while a male grizzly of Denali Park in interior Alaska would be considered a giant at six hundred pounds (272 kg), males living along the coast often weigh twice that. Standing erect on hind legs, an adult Kodiak bear can tower ten feet (3 m) or better above the ground. Between seven thousand and eight thousand bears are believed to live along the Alaskan shoreline and on the so-called ABC coastal islands—Admiralty, Baranof, and Chichagof—from the border of British Columbia to the tip of the Alaskan Peninsula.

Through my experiences with these mammoth animals, I am convinced that brown bears are different from inland grizzlies in other important ways. I believe that they are less irritable, and they also seem more confident. Credit it to an easier life, a higher standard of living—whatever. I personally feel more comfortable photographing the Kodiak bears than the

eat, while the other bear races off, away from us. As I stand in the wet sand witnessing this incredible action, I realize that we have not shot a single picture.

Luckily, this is not our last chance to photograph the bears. Throughout the morning, an incoming tide carries schools of humpback salmon into the small stream. From close range we are able to shoot photos of the fishing bears as fast as we can load and reload film into our motor-driven cameras. Not once during

An old male brownie stands in the same favorite fishing spot it has held for several summers at the McNeil River State Game Sanctuary, Alaska.

Near the mouth of the McNeil River, a lone bear studies the cold current for any sign of salmon surging upstream.

grizzlies. They seem to be more predictable and less adversarial.

ON THE TRAIL OF THE BROWN BEAR

Our journey to Hallo Bay to photograph the fishing bears really began in Homer, Alaska, far down the Kenai Peninsula southwest of Anchorage. We loaded our photo gear (and little else) into a Kachemak Air floatplane and taxied out into Cook Inlet. The pilot, Bill DeCreeft, flew us out to a rendezvous on the water with the *Waters*. To get to the boat, we flew ninety minutes over one of the last and largest pure wildernesses left on earth. From the outskirts of Anchorage to Cold Bay, where the Alaskan mainland ends, there are no permanent, year-round human settlements. This vast, primeval region still belongs to the whales and

eagles, the sea lions and sea birds, and, in the summer, the brown bears. We flew past steaming, volcanic Augustine Island, past Cape Douglas and the McNeil River State Game Sanctuary, to Kukak Bay, where the *Waters*, a former Army tugboat and National Geographic Society research vessel, was waiting for us. Photographers Bob and Evelyn Mauck of Worthington, Ohio, were already aboard. As night fell, we could just make out the dark shapes of brown bears on shore. But by daybreak rain was pelting down, and we were completely socked in by fog.

In dreary weather for two long days, we cruised from Kukak to Kaflia and Kinak Bays, passing Takli Island and Amalik Bay, then motoring through a scenic channel into Geographic Harbor. En route we passed sea lion haulouts where kittiwakes and glau-

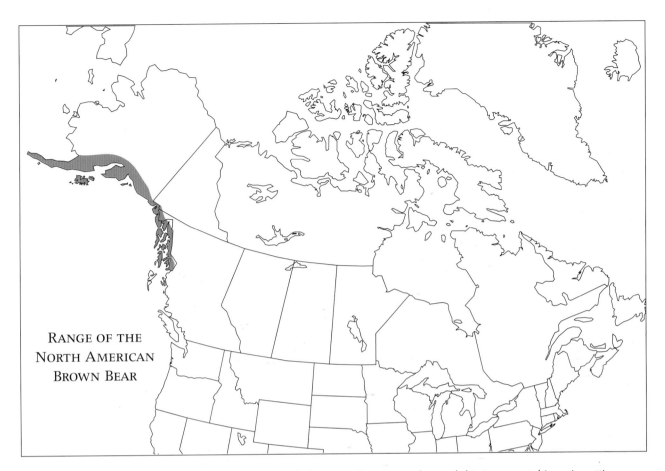

RANGE OF THE
NORTH AMERICAN
BROWN BEAR

Facing page: *The huge adult brown bears are not fighting, as it appears. Instead this is a courtship pair getting acquainted at Hallo Bay. Brownie courtship can be very rough.*

cous-winged gulls screamed overhead. We counted orcas, and porpoises occasionally swam in the bow waves of the *Waters*. But brown bears were not numerous, until we dropped anchor in the lee of Ninagiak Island and later in Hallo Bay, where the shoreline was alive with brownies.

What an absolutely primitive and spectacular scene it was. Kukak Volcano, snowbound Mount Steller, and Hallo Glacier loomed behind the bears, which were digging clams in the sand and capturing pink salmon in the numerous small streams along the shore. Not long after our arrival a pale summer sun broke through the overcast sky.

The first bear we observed was a young female, which Evelyn nicknamed Dolly. Dolly seemed thinner than the other bears, and she was inept at catching salmon. But she was determined, and her spirited and rapid pursuit of salmon was difficult to follow through a viewfinder.

Abruptly, Dolly ran away from us. We soon real-ized her hasty retreat was due to two bears approaching behind us. But the bears were not interested in us at all, and, bounding and huffing side by side, they ran right past us and splashed into the same stream where Dolly had been fishing. They, however, paid no attention to the fish. This was a courting pair. Evelyn named these two lovers Fred and Ginger. The two did seem to move as gracefully as Astaire and Rogers, to the music of a silent orchestra.

COURTSHIP AND MATING

Brown bear courtship is a very athletic and rough undertaking. Fred and Ginger danced, chased, pawed, boxed, and bit one another, often when standing up on their hind feet. The performance continued for nearly an hour, as we exposed numerous rolls of film. An incoming tide flooded the area, but the bears continued their antics.

Throughout the frolicking, the lovers paid little attention to our cluster of photographers. Suddenly,

A male brown bear approaches a fishing site slowly on the McNeil River. It was the loser in a dominance battle. Notice the ugly open wound on its shoulder.

something caused Fred to stop and stare at us. He did not seem happy with what he saw, and he began to stalk in our direction. For a few moments it seemed that the gulls ceased to scream and the wind suddenly died as Fred approached far too close for comfort—my comfort, anyway. But just as suddenly as he had approached, he stopped and turned to see Ginger running rapidly in the other direction. Love won out. The big male turned and followed her while we drew in a collective deep breath.

The next day Fred and Ginger were back in amorous action on the beach, but apparently the mutual ardor was cooling somewhat; the bears mixed a little fishing and dining with their frolicking. On the third day Ginger was gone, and we came upon Fred sleeping on his back in a bed excavated out of the gravelly shore. He had a deep red gash in his foreleg, a souvenir of the affair.

Despite such wounds, except for a mother's attention to her cubs, the closest thing to tenderness among brown bears occurs, at intervals and if they are alone, between mating pairs. The radio-tracking of collared bears indicates that these duos are not always as rough as Fred and Ginger, particularly when no competing bears are around.

Mating takes place from late May into July throughout the brown bear's range; during this time females are receptive for only one to two weeks. Females first breed when they are from five to seven years old and will breed every third year throughout their lives. Males travel far to find receptive sows, and some male bears stay with the females throughout their entire estrus period. However, both sexes are polygamous. Alaskan biologist Larry Aumiller recalls one dominant male that copulated with five females during one long day.

After copulation, the fertilized egg floats freely in the female uterus until late autumn, when she looks for a hibernation site. The egg is not implanted in the wall of the uterus, where development of the young

A yearling cub crowds close to its mother beside the McNeil River. There are several boars in the vicinity to be avoided.

begins, until November. Tiny, helpless cubs are born two to three months later. In proportion to the mother's weight, these brownie cubs are smaller at birth than those of most other mammals.

MOTHER AND CUBS

In many children's books, furry little cubs live playful, carefree lives, always protected by devoted and, if necessary, avenging mothers. This is generally true, although young first-time mothers might be more timid and less protective than older ones. More experienced bears often develop a hair-trigger temper to add potency to their claws, jaws, muscles, and terrible teeth. As long as her cubs remain underfoot or very

near, they are for the most part safe. Most mothers, although not all, are fierce defenders of their cubs until they and their young separate when the cubs are two and a half years old. Still, the death toll of brown bear cubs is high; almost 50 percent do not survive their first year. As with black and inland grizzly bears, male bears are often the culprits.

Every year, cubs arrive on the McNeil River State Game Sanctuary on the Alaska Peninsula with their mothers, and a certain number do not walk away again when August blends into September. Inevitably, a few are washed away in the strong current, and many are captured by males fishing farther downstream. In addition, sanctuary manager Aumiller believes that

At dusk a mother leads her three cubs across the lagoon at the mouth of the McNeil River. They are heading for the salmon spawning areas upstream.

brown bear mothers have trouble counting; some may not even realize a cub is missing. But this can work both ways. One mother arrived at the river in July with twins, and a few days later was being trailed by four cubs. Some young may not be able to recognize their own mothers, and the cubs will sometimes attach themselves to any other female that does not drive them away. Females do recognize their own cubs, but some seem willing to nurse, and even to adopt for a short time, any lonely cub that follows persistently and bawls loudly enough.

SIZE

Brown bears are the largest of all carnivorous land mammals. They average roughly the same size as polar bears. Of all land mammals only elephants, hippos, and rhinos are heavier. The largest known brown bear skull (now in the Los Angeles County Museum) measures 30 12/16 inches according to the Boone and Crockett scoring system. Sixteen other brown bear skulls measure more than the largest polar bear skull, which measured 29 15/16. However, no one can state with absolute authority that either the brown or the polar bear is the more massive. One polar bear specimen that is now in the Carnegie Museum was cut up and the pieces weighed after it was shot. Even with the body fluids lost, the animal weighed 1,728 pounds (784 kg). It might have weighed almost a ton (907 kg) when still alive. Brown bears reach their greatest size on Kodiak Island, and North American brown bears often are mistakenly called Kodiak bears, regardless of where they live. On average, adult male brownies will measure four to four and a half feet (1.2–1.4 m) at the shoulder and weigh six hundred to eight hundred pounds (272–363 kg). Females on average are slightly smaller.

DIET

When brown bears emerge from their hibernation dens in spring after months of fasting, they gorge on a tonic of newly emergent grasses, such as skunk cabbage,

hellebore, cow parsnip, and the tender shoots of many other green, succulent plants. At this time the plants have peak protein content,

But in the summertime, brown bears tend to be meat-eaters much more so than inland grizzlies, no doubt because meat is much more available where they live. Brown bears have been seen stalking such large mammals as blacktailed deer, moose, and caribou, as well as Dall's sheep. They usually take young or winter-weakened animals. They also dig out ground squirrels and marmots from underground dens and rip apart beaver houses to get the home-builders living inside.

But despite great strength and speed afoot, remarkable attributes for such a large animal, brown bears have not evolved into efficient predators as mountain lions have. They are not fast or stealthy enough to catch healthy, adult big game animals that have keen senses. Nor do they cooperate in hunting, as wolves do. However, browns do not need to be skilled, deadly predators, living as they do among the abundant food choices at the edge of the sea. For example, we observed those Hallo Bay bears digging clams when salmon were not yet running. When one food source dried up, they simply moved on to another option.

Roy Randall, a veteran bear guide on Afognak Island, near Kodiak Island, told me about some resourceful and motivated brown bears swimming from Afognak far out to a satellite island where sea birds nest, in order to gorge on eggs and young birds. During another Alaskan excursion to Glacier Bay in the southeastern panhandle, Peggy and I watched a female prowling the rocky shoreline with twin cubs. Through a spotting scope, we could tell that the sow was scraping mussels from the rocks at water's edge with foreclaws and teeth. The little ones tried to imitate her for a while, but gave up and pestered their mother until she stopped long enough to nurse them.

Dead whales, harbor seals, or sea lions that wash ashore can be a bonanza for bears; they will linger and feed until the last edible matter is gone. One summer Roy Randall watched a bear feed on a Steller's sea lion carcass that a rising tide and strong current threatened to carry away. But the bear dragged the carcass, which weighed more than twice as much as itself, up a steep gravel bank and over a waist-high driftwood

barrier to a spot where it could dine in peace.

THE IMPORTANCE OF SALMON

Despite the marine life and other prey available, many Alaskan brown bears depend on the annual spawning runs of the state's five species of salmon for most of their protein. The brown bears growth, their health, their preparation for winter, the size of their litters, even their own survival hinges on the salmon.

Salmon spend almost their entire lives in saltwater, but eventually they return to spawn and to die in the same sweetwater streams where they hatched. There are hundreds of streams draining southwestern Alaska, and all five kinds of salmon spawn here at predictable times and in fairly predictable numbers. Even the smallest spawning runs attract at least a few bears. Other streams with heavier, longer-lasting spawning runs attract large numbers of bears. Instinct seems to guide bears to the streams exactly when the first schools of fish arrive. One of the greatest of the brown bear waterways, and certainly the best area for viewing bears, is the McNeil River, on the lonely Alaska Peninsula, not far from where we watched the

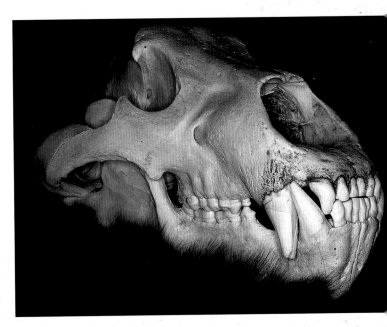

Above: *The bleached skull of a brown bear reveals the long canine teeth imbedded in powerful jaws.*

Facing page: *A giant brown male finishes a salmon just a short distance from the photography blind above the McNeil River.*

Above: *Early in summer, when the new green grasses are full of nutrition, a brown bear becomes a busy eating machine, often around the clock.*

Right: *Old, well-worn bear trails wind through fireweed meadows that lead to fishing and clamming beaches of Shelikof Strait, Katmai National Park, Alaska.*

love dancing of Fred and Ginger.

The waters of the McNeil originate from snow melting in the mountains that form the spine of the Alaska Peninsula. On rare sunny days the glistening mountains are an exquisite backdrop for a river that rushes and tumbles, as clear as the air, through meadows of wild parsnip and waist-high, sub-arctic grasses and willow, all swaying back and forth in the damp, salty wind from the sea. By midsummer, lupine and other wildflowers color the banks of the McNeil. Not far above the tidal flats and its confluence with the

Shelikof Strait, the river cuts through a final rocky ledge and thunders over a series of falls, cascading down to a deep pool at the base. In that pool below the falls, salmon mass to rest before proceeding, or trying to proceed, upstream. This place is a wild sight unlike any other in the world, one of the finest of all wildlife spectacles.

The fish, primarily chum (or dog) salmon, are fat and vigorous from a lifetime of living at sea. But they pause below the falls anyway, as if gathering more strength before surging upward and onward through

the powerful current. The brief sojourn of the salmon just below those falls, someone said, seems almost like a death wish; beginning in July, bears station themselves all around this stretch of the river to pounce on them, just as they have done for centuries. They come to the falls from as far as thirty miles (48 km) away. As many as sixty-eight bears (in 1990) have been counted in and around the McNeil Falls area at one time. That same day, a total of 107 different bears were seen in the vicinity. Many more visit the area at least briefly sometime during the peak of the salmon run.

Peggy and I have been extremely lucky to join the bears at the McNeil River State Game Sanctuary four times. The one-hundred-square-mile (260-sq-km) area, which is protected from any hunting, also is shielded from unlimited, random visitation by people. Access is by permit only, and recipients are determined through an annual lottery. Only ten winners at a time, for a period of four days each, are allowed to visit this section of the McNeil River during July and August, when the fish are running. All visitors must camp in one designated campsite near the river's mouth, and

This adult brownie knows *there are salmon lurking in the shallows all around. But he must pinpoint their exact location then pounce!*

there are daily group treks to the one platform site above the McNeil Falls where bear watching is permitted. If all that seems unduly restrictive, keep in mind that during the past twenty years there have been no people-bear incidents at the McNeil River Sanctuary, even though the two come into close daily contact.

The long-time manager of the McNeil River Sanctuary system is the dedicated biologist and bears' best friend, Larry Aumiller, who has become almost as much a part of the place as the animals. No one person has spent as much time watching and studying brown bears than this dedicated man. During a lifetime of roaming national and state refuges, I have never met a game manager who handles a delicate and potentially dangerous job so well. Peggy and I have made the one-and-a-half-mile hike from the campsite to the McNeil Falls many times with Aumiller and have met many bears along the way. All have been exciting experiences that we could match nowhere else.

Brown bears, like all of the world's bears, tend to be loners much of the time. A few, according to popular literature, seem to wander through life with chips on their shoulders. But along the lower McNeil, when the salmon are surging upstream and a gathering of only twenty bears is small, it is apparent that they can get along with one another, even if they do not exactly share equally in the bounty. Since this annual fish feast lasts only a few weeks, the visiting bears must be occupied much of the time with obtaining food and eating it, rather than fighting over it. So a sort of truce—an uneasy peace at times—goes into effect.

SOCIAL HIERARCHY

While watching the bears at McNeil River, it is immediately obvious that some kind of accepted fishing etiquette or protocol must exist to keep the river banks from developing into a bear battlefield. On most days fishing takes place from afternoon until dusk and later, although humans are never allowed to linger beyond late afternoon. Sometimes the fishing and feeding by the bears goes on all day, depending on how many salmon have entered the river. There is almost always great competition for the limited fishing space available.

Derek Stonerov is one of the biologists who have

A male sockeye salmon in brilliant spawning color ventures into very shallow water, following a female. It's very vulnerable to bears here.

long observed the McNeil bears. To learn about bear coexistence, he observed and recorded three thousand separate bear-with-bear encounters in the water or on the river bank. Stonerov defined an "encounter" as a meeting in which two or more bears meet and react in an unfriendly way. By carefully noting which bear won and which one lost each encounter, the researcher eventually had enough information to determine that there was a definite ursine hierarchy, and that the social system worked exceedingly well.

According to Stonerov, trouble among bears can be precipitated by any of four main causes. Competition for a choice fishing spot was the most common one. Violation of the distance or tolerance level of another bear was second. The arrival of a strange bear whose position on the ranking scale was yet to be determined was third. The fourth cause was something that biologists call redirected aggression, that is when one bear loses an encounter and takes out its anger and frustration on a third innocent individual. Dis-

putes that could not be solved by posturing or bluffing would erupt into short, sharp, physical confrontations that established the relative ranking of the competing bears throughout the salmon fishing season.

As with inland grizzlies and many other mammals, the social hierarchy of McNeil brown bears is based on size, sex, and reproductive condition. All the bears in one category normally give ground to any bears in a higher-ranking grouping. Individuals may be most aggressive with others in their own group, as ranking within categories is not as well defined.

The top classification is composed of the largest and oldest (up to a point) males. Larry Aumiller noted for us how these large, powerful, dominant boars not only stake out and defend the best fishing sites, but claim those same sites for several seasons in a row until a bigger, stronger male ousts them. Aumiller's detailed notes confirm that one super-male would tolerate no competition near his spot for twelve of the twenty-

Red roe squirts from the body of chum salmon just captured by a bear fishing on the McNeil River.

four summers the bear was known to visit McNeil.

The second highest-ranking group is composed of females with cubs. Next come the sibling groups that travel together, fish in comparative peace, and pretty much cooperate in their fishing. Smaller, unattached males and females are at the bottom of the McNeil River hierarchy, and probably wherever else a large congregation of bears exists. This final category is the only one with a somewhat well-defined social hierarchy within the group, as males tend to outclass females. But age and size also are factors.

Within the second highest group (mothers with cubs), the age of the young may well determine the sow's ranking. Females with yearlings (or older) cubs can afford to be more aggressive than females with "spring cubs," those born only a few months earlier.

The older the cubs, the more likely they are to imitate and stand up beside their mother when facing trouble. Younger cubs tend to be fearful, and their mothers invest much time simply defending them. But no matter how defensive and careful the sows, a summer does not pass in which older bears fail to catch, kill, and eat an unlucky or careless cub or two. It is a horrifying thing to watch, although no more so than the scenes of humans killing other humans presented every night on prime-time television.

Stonerov noted that a good many mothers defend their cubs to the point of going on the offensive. Females sometimes savagely charge other bears, even much larger males, that come too close to their young, even if the male's approach is inadvertent. More often the less aggressive and wiser mothers hustle the cubs

In the cold water just below the McNeil River falls, a bear relishes the last bites of a fresh-run salmon caught nearby.

true not only in arctic Canada, but here as well. A bear walking in this manner was either looking for or expecting trouble.

The Dene knew, and now I did too, that to judge a bear's mood you should watch the position of its head. With short tails and long hair, brown and grizzly bears cannot send signals through body language as well as some other mammals. But their heads, necks, and mouths convey their intentions. Based on my own observations, coastal brown bears seem to walk with their heads held higher than their inland grizzly cousins, indicating a less aggressive nature. The thousands of bear photographs in our files tend to confirm this.

The bears also send messages by crouching and circling, bluffing and looking away, yawning and feigning disinterest, backing up while still facing a rival, standing motionless and seeming to stare through another bear, and sitting down. Low-ranking bears may approach much larger animals on their stomachs in a submissive manner. Sometimes these bears even get away with stealing the fish of the dominant bear from this lowly position.

well out of harm's way at the first indication of possible trouble.

After thousands of hours of brown bear observation on the McNeil River, Aumiller realized that the bear hierarchy can subtly change. Also, concessions are sometimes made. A dominant boar may be far less tolerant of an upcoming rival than of an inferior bear that is not a threat to its standing. Another bear, sleepy and with a stomach full of salmon, may briefly be more tolerant of a subordinate bear, which, without a good fishing spot of its own, encroaches on the dominant bear's feeding area. Altogether, the McNeil animals, creatures that are basically anti-social by nature, manage to get along surprisingly well with a minimum amount of conflict or injury during this crucial time of year.

TELLING MOOD THROUGH BODY SIGNS

During a long ago fishing trip to northern Canada, a Yellowknife Dene Indian, whose face and upper arms were scarred from an encounter with a barren ground grizzly, told me that the bear to always watch was the one that walked slowly, swaying a little, with its head held down lower than its shoulder hump. One afternoon at McNeil, I realized that this observation held

PERSONALITY

Along the McNeil River and other major salmon spawning streams, the distinctive character of individual bears is evident. No two stalk fish in exactly the same manner, and some are much more successful than others. Some animals are extremely patient, standing motionless for long periods in cold, shallow eddies watching for a suitable fish to appear. In the shallows, the bears can trap salmon against the gravel streambed with forepaws, then lift the squirming catch from the water with powerful jaws. Other bears use the submarine tactic, face deep in the water, eyes apparently open, waiting for a hapless fish to appear.

In Katmai National Park, which borders the McNeil River State Game Sanctuary, some bears have learned to position themselves above the Brooks River Falls in precisely the right places to catch sockeye salmon in mid-air as they leap the falls to reach spawning beds farther upstream. On the American River just outside Katmai's boundaries, I once watched a seemingly lazy bruin lie flat on its belly in the swift, icy current, with eyes and snout down almost to water level. From that unlikely position it would suddenly

Well below the best fishing sites on the McNeil River, dominated by males, a mother with cubs watches for a chance to catch a salmon.

uncoil and come up onto its feet, grasping a salmon. This particular bear was very wasteful. On shore it would eat only part of a salmon, generally the rich, red roe, before ambushing another. Gulls and a family of gray wolves lurking in the willows would eat the leftovers. Earlier I had watched the same wolves trying to catch fish for themselves, but compared to any of the local bears, they were inept.

Some brown bears fish very aggressively, like Dolly of Hallo Bay, racing up and down a stream and frequently lunging or diving unsuccessfully after any darting shadows they see. I have watched other bears swimming and exploring deep pools and finally diving for dead or injured fish on the bottom. A good many bears that never become adept at fishing survive by scavenging partly eaten carcasses that lay on the river bank. Some higher ranking bears intimidate and hijack fish from inferiors. One of the most serious bear clashes I ever saw on the McNeil River began when one large bear tried to take a fish from a bear

that did not acknowledge its inferior status. While the two fought, a third bear disappeared with the disputed salmon.

Larry Aumiller has noted that, techniques and temperamental differences aside, age and experience tend to produce better fishing skills. Older bears usually are able to spend more time relishing their nutritious meals and waste less time catching them. Younger bears use up more energy for the calories they realize.

KATMAI NATIONAL PARK

Another outstanding place to watch brown bears is the strange and stark Katmai National Park, which can accommodate more visitors than the nearby McNeil River.

For five days in June 1912, violent earthquakes gave warning of what would be one of the greatest volcanic explosions in modern history at Novarupta Volcano within Katmai Park. White-hot ash started to pour from fissures in the earth. Then, within a few

Patches

Like the Craighead brothers in Yellowstone and bear biologists elsewhere, Larry Aumiller has given human names to many of the bears at McNeil. There was Ladybird, an irritable and high-strung female; Whitey, a very active, but inept fisherman; Red, White, and Blue, cubs first seen on the Fourth of July; Woofie; Earl; Flashman; Luther; The Black Brothers; and Charlie Brown, one of the top bears for many years. One female, Gold, had gone Hollywood, with long, yellow claws, which frequently glinted in the sunlight. And of course there was Patches.

A long dominant male bear named Patches by biologists approaches a personal fishing hole along the McNeil River. The animal probably suffers from arthritis.

When I first saw Patches, a huge, ragged-looking male veteran of many McNeil summers, he was already sixteen years old and king of his side of the river. Patches would confidently, almost arrogantly, stroll onto the scene late in the morning, and the other bears would give him a clear path. If a bear happened to be fishing in Patches's spot, it quickly vacated. Patches never seemed to work very diligently at his fishing, but he more than made up for his general lack of industriousness with occasional, bewildering bursts of speed and agility. One typical day he caught twenty salmon, averaging about six pounds (2.7 kg) apiece, without missing a strike. He ate most of the fish entirely, but consumed only the ripe, red eggs of the last few, leaving the remainder for the gulls and bald eagles to finish.

Despite these seemingly impressive numbers of salmon and his considerable bulk, Patches was not the champion glutton on the river. Many other bears have been observed catching twenty or more salmon in one stretch. In 1987, Groucho, a dark, long-legged bear, set the record for a single day by any one bear by catching and eating ninety salmon. Over the course of the year, Groucho caught a total of 1,012 fish, another remarkable record.

The last time I saw Patches, he was twenty-four years old and looked it. The old arrogance was gone. He walked very slowly and seemed to suffer from arthritis, which does afflict old bears. Other bears no longer gave him as much respect as they had in the past. After catching a few salmon, Patches would fall asleep right beside his fishing hole, the way an old man might doze in front of the television after a heavy Sunday dinner. During his fitful naps, the other bears edged closer than they would have dared in earlier years. Perhaps the old, snoozing codger dreamed of past romances and of the many other bears on the river that he had sired. No doubt one of these would soon drive the twelve-hundred-pound (544 kg) Patches from the dominant position he held for almost two decades.

Facing page: At low tide along the south shore of the Alaska Peninsula, a single bear searches for clam beds to excavate.

Both photos: *When male brown bears of similar size and stature meet along a trail, there is usually a good bit of posturing, grimacing and greeting, as with these two.*

minutes, two and a half cubic miles (10.25 km^3) of ash blasted into the sky and swept down adjacent valleys like giant tidal waves. Trees were snapped off and carbonized by blasts of scorching wind. When the violence ended, more than forty square miles (105 sq km) of Katmai were buried beneath a layer of ash as deep as seven hundred feet (213 m). Katmai had become a flat, pale landscape stretching to the horizon, without a sign of vegetation or animal life. Although the main eruption was over, countless small vents continued to spout steam into the still air. The area was aptly named the Valley of Ten Thousand Smokes.

Today, the thermal activity has ended, but the park is stunningly beautiful and is inhabited by wolves and wolverines, snowshoe hares and lemmings, mink, martens, and river otters. Every summer, salmon swarm into the wilderness rivers of Katmai, such as the Brooks. Brown bears, at the top of the food chain here as elsewhere, arrive on schedule to dine on them. No readily accessible wildlife refuge in the world outclasses Katmai.

My first meeting with Katmai's bears occurred just below the steep falls of the Brooks River, a site that is similar to the falls of the McNeil River. In 1960, my son Bob and I were flycasting for rainbow trout, and the first few sockeye salmon to arrive in the river were darting beneath the falls. The fishing was fast, and I forgot everything else. I looked over at Bob who, waist deep in the water, had hooked a high-jumping rainbow. Also watching the action intently was a large, dripping brown bear that stood no more than thirty feet (9 m) behind him. The roar of the falls had muffled the sound of its approach. Suddenly, Bob saw the bear too, broke off his line and waded slowly to shore, far out of the bear's path. From then on, we carefully watched over our shoulders while we fished.

I often think how that bear could easily have had a much larger meal than the swift salmon it later caught. Fortunately, most brown bears regard people either as inedible parts of the landscape or objects to avoid at all costs. But this is not always the case.

At about the same time Bob and I were fishing the rivers of Katmai, an amateur but experienced wildlife photographer, Jay Reeves, pitched his tent on the bank of Frosty Creek in the Izembek National Wildlife Refuge, at the tip of the Alaska Peninsula just west of Katmai and the McNeil River. A year earlier, another man, Pat Wren, had mysteriously disappeared in this same area. Some thought he drowned; others believed he was the victim of a bear attack. Wren's remains were never found.

The day after Jay Reeves set up camp, a federal biologist flying a helicopter survey spotted the man's headless body below. Refuge personnel hurried to the spot and shot a medium-sized, male brown bear. The bruin's stomach contained human flesh and bones, as well as part of a pack of cigarettes. Reeves had made one fatal mistake by locating his camp right beside an active bear trail.

Later, I met biologist Ed Bailey who had once been stationed at Izembek Refuge and was familiar with the Reeves incident. Bailey had spent much of his life in outermost Alaska observing bears and, within his own experience, Bailey could recall no other cases of brown bears killing and eating people. In the Reeves case, hunger did not seem to be the reason for the attack; an ample crop of berries was ripening in the area at the time, and salmon were spawning not far away.

In recent years the numbers of visitors hoping to see brown bears at Katmai has greatly increased. The Park Service deserves credit for the fact that no serious incidents have happened in this place where so many people meet so many bears. For example, it is no longer permitted to fish right among the bears as Bob and I had once done. As at McNeil, rangers built a bear-viewing platform to concentrate bear watchers in one place above the bear's fishing activities. All visitors to Katmai must first view an orientation movie on how to behave among bears.

THE KODIAK BEARS

Like Katmai National Park and the McNeil River Sanctuary, the Kodiak National Wildlife Refuge, where the largest of all brown bears roam, offers outstanding opportunities to see bears. This vast, splendid refuge covers three thousand square miles (7,800 sq km) of the southwestern two-thirds of Kodiak Island, plus a much smaller unit on adjacent Afognak Island. The climate is wet, unpredictable, and surprisingly mild; even winter temperatures rarely fall below zero (-18 °C). Summers tend to be cool, and clouds obscure

the sun 70 percent of the time. Kodiak is hauntingly beautiful, a rugged escape for anyone who genuinely relishes wilderness—and seeing bears.

During the summer, the interior of Kodiak Island is covered with dense, verdant vegetation. Sedges and fireweed as tall as a person mix with salmonberry, blueberry, and wild rose. Scattered dense thickets of willow, elderberry, and alder dot the greenery. Stay clear of the sharp thorns of the red-berried devil's club, which also grows head-high. There are heathland knolls high up in the mountains, which rise to four thousand feet (1,220 m). Below the peaks, there are seven major watersheds, with large lakes, bogs, salt flats, soggy meadows, and clear rivers that run pink or red with salmon in summertime. It is a nearly perfect mosaic for brown bears. Although there is a greater density of brown bears on Admiralty Island in southeastern Alaska than anywhere else, the bears of Kodiak Island average much heavier and might equal the Admiralty biomass.

Many consider—justifiably—the Kodiak bear, *Ursus arctos middendorfi,* the greatest trophy animal on earth, and scientifically regulated hunting does take place on Kodiak Island. The revenue from hunting, together with that from summertime bear watching, has become the most important source of income for the island's economy. It would seem reasonable to protect this bear bonanza, this matchless treasure, at all costs. Unfortunately, the opposite is too often true.

Above: *Some of the wildest coasts in the world are in southwestern Alaska. This scene is of Kaflia Bay on Shelikof Strait where eagles nest and brown bears often prowl.*

Top left: *When the fishing is good, an adult brown bear can eat ten or more chum salmon such as this one, without taking a break.*

Above and left: *These brown bears are searching the shallow mouth of a small stream for incoming salmon. When one spots a fish, it begins the rush to catch a meal, even if straight toward a nervous cameraman.*

One of twin brown bear cubs wants to play, but its mother has her eye on more important matters: salmon spawning in the nearby stream.

In the 1960s, Jim Rearden, in an article in *Outdoor Life* magazine, exposed an ugly bear-killing operation on Kodiak. The animals were being shot with automatic rifles mounted military-style on small aircraft. Conservation-minded hunters were shocked by such a wholesale slaughter, but the aerial shooting would continue for some time.

What precipitated the killing was nothing new in North America at that time or today: conflict between livestock, ranchers, and predators. Brown bears began to prey on island livestock when the first Russian settlers brought cattle to Kodiak around 1795. Ever since, ranchers have been battling the bears with rifles, traps, snares, lye, packs of dogs, and poisons. During the 1930s, rancher Tom Nelson, by his own admission, destroyed 115 bears with the help of a pack of redbone hounds.

A terrible mistake was made when the Kodiak National Wildlife Refuge was established in 1941: The federal government did not include all of the unsettled parts of the island. Instead, the government leased the northeastern third of the island to cattle ranchers, even though raising livestock on Kodiak was a very marginal business, as it is today. One rancher, who eventually threw in the towel and quit raising livestock on the island, said it would have been easier and more sensible to run cattle in New York's Central Park than on Kodiak. Even so, until the 1960s ranchers were showing some restraint, killing only bears that preyed on their cattle on their own leased land. After all, these bears were trophies that, at the time, were worth at least $3,000 each (about $7,500 in the mid-1990s) to the islanders in guiding, lodging, and other fees. In other words, the bears were worth much more to the economy than all the beefsteak they could eat.

In the 1960s, ranchers claimed that bear damage was suddenly increasing and asked for government help. They even requested a supply of the deadly poison 1080, used so effectively against coyotes, wolves, and other "vermin" elsewhere in the West. Rancher

An old, well-worn bear trail follows this lonely shore on Afognak Island Alaska, the home of a large population of brownies.

Joe Zentner mounted an M-1 rifle on his Piper aircraft and, without publicity, escalated the bear war. Others caught on and mounted powerful rifles on aircraft. The airborne strafers left numerous bear carcasses to rot across Kodiak Island.

Experienced military combat pilots were hired, and the toll of bears mounted. Veteran Kodiak outfitters and hunting guides charge that the pilots were gunning down bears as far as twenty miles (32 km) beyond ranch leases and into the National Wildlife Refuge itself. The aerial shooting ended in 1970, only after international attention focused on the airborne gunners.

There is no way to ever know exactly how many Kodiak bears were destroyed in the aerial campaigns or by other means of slaughter. No official figures have ever been released, but an Alaska Department of Fish and Game biologist told me off the record that at least two thousand "marauding" bears had been dispatched by ranchers in the previous thirty years. Some of the

bears were culprits, many were not. That amounts to a loss of about fifteen million dollars (in 1995 dollars) to Kodiak Island's economy. Despite the obvious financial effect and the international protest, the conflict between the bears and the ranchers on Kodiak Island remains a controversial, emotional issue that simmers just under the surface.

BROWN BEARS IN THE PANHANDLE

It is much more pleasant to turn to brown bears some distance away, on Admiralty, Chichagof, and other islands off the southeastern Alaskan coast, a region often called the Panhandle. In this area, dense vegetation resulting from very heavy rainfall makes passage difficult or even impossible. Even with a bear's strength, the forest can be tough going unless the bear follows forest "highways" made by other bears that have walked the same route in the past.

Most of these trails are ancient, traditional pathways used by the bears to commute between ocean shores, where they forage at the water's edge, through nearly impenetrable brush to beyond the timberline. Familiar side trails or pathways lead to bogs, where skunk cabbage and other edibles flourish, and to grassy openings where the bears also graze. Not only have generations of bears used these same pathways, but the bears living there today have stepped in their own footprints trip after trip.

Bears defecate as they walk, without pausing, and the brown bears in this region are no different. Many other species benefit greatly from such bear habits, most notably the native Sitka blacktailed deer, which also make use of the bear trails. Even a brown bear of medium size can eat eighty to ninety pounds (36–41 kg) of vegetation (often including berries) in a day's time. Since each bear leaves behind a trail of scats, and each scat contains intact berry seeds (and plenty of fertilizer), a wandering brown bear plants miniature gardens wherever it goes. The deer depend on the fertile berry gardens for food. In springtime, the seed sowers—the Johnny Appleseeds of Alaska—might catch a blacktail fawn or two in repayment for establishing the food plots.

Brown bears are a part of the cycle of nature wherever they live. At the tail end of a float trip on the Alsek River from the Yukon to tidewater Alaska, Peggy and I saw riverside trees from which bears had clawed and stripped ribbons of bark. Some of this activity may have been for territorial marking, but the animals and their cubs also seemed to be licking sap, especially that of the yellow cedar. This is not good for the health of an individual tree, because it allows fungi and insects to invade the trunks. But in time, cavities form in which birds and small mammals nest before the whole tree falls, rots, and is recycled.

Throughout its Alaskan range, the brown bear is more than just a magnificent creation of nature, it is also a creature on which many others depend, and a symbol of the last greatest wilderness on earth.

Above: *In the yellow light of morning, a young brown bear is already watching for the first school of salmon to enter an Alaskan stream from saltwater.*

Overleaf: *At low tide in Glacier Bay National Park, a mother brown bear teaches cubs to scrape mussels from the shoreline at low tide. A second cub is not interested.*

The Future of the North American Bear

Late one August afternoon, a black bear emerges from a woods near where a residential street deadends on the outskirts of rapidly growing Boulder, Colorado. It sniffs the air, hesitates, and then walks directly toward a pile of trash that someone has dumped in an area cleared for a new home. The voices of playing children are audible not far from where the animal finds half of a ripe watermelon and begins to eat.

Before the bear is finished, two boys on bicycles ride up, and the bruin rushes at them. One of the boys falls from his bike, screams, and runs, but the bear does not pursue. There is plenty to eat in the trash. Thirty or so minutes later a team from the Colorado Division of Wildlife arrives, and they shoot the bear with a tranquilizing dart. Before they load the limp animal into a pickup truck and transport it far from the temptations of a city, they affix a red tag to one ear.

Tagging that bear is like booking and fingerprinting a human prowler at the police station. The animal now has a record as a nuisance or garbage bear. This bear is given a reprieve, just this once. In years past, before being destroyed as incorrigible, problem bears in Colorado might be moved several times in the hope that they would kick their garbage eating habits. But times have changed.

Today there are many more invasions into bear territory by suburbia, campgrounds, and other human habitats than there were just a decade ago. Consequently, that red-tagged ear on the watermelon-eating bear marks it as a first-time offender.

This old veteran of many summers on salmon streams
requires vast wilderness areas to survive.

The Division of Wildlife has determined that such bears get only one chance. The second time red-tagged bears are caught, they are killed "for the public safety." Two strikes and the bear is out. During the summer of 1994, at least thirty-three black bears were killed in Colorado under this policy.

The problem of bears roaming through towns is likely to get worse. In states with rapidly growing human populations, such as Colorado, Washington, and Oregon, which also have large black bear populations, people are clearing land, building homes, and moving ever deeper into bear country. In Colorado, the human population of eight counties has doubled since 1970. Douglas County, just south of Denver, has grown by almost 900 percent, and a lot of that sprawl has been into what was once fine black bear country. In addition, the total area of the popular Vail and Beaver Creek ski resorts has grown by about 450 percent in the same period.

With the suburban expansion has also come the inevitable increase in "bear scare" stories. During the early 1990s, bears have invaded Boy Scout camps and trailer parks, tree nurseries, vegetable gardens, back-yard barbecues, and at least one all-night convenience store. They keep coming because the human expansion means more garbage to rummage through. The bears can find everything from inadequate disposal facilities to general carelessness, such as leaving a bowl of dog food out on the back porch. Executive director Matt Reid of the Montana-based Great Bear Foundation points out that "bears just cannot resist the unnatural bounty that is out there and available to them." People are swiftly, inexorably taking over bear territory, not only in the western United States, but almost everywhere bears live outside the public lands of North America. Even within public lands, the human encroachment is deep and all encompassing. There are over 400,000 miles (640,000 km) of roads in our national forests, eight times the mileage of the entire U.S. Interstate highway system. Many more roads are under construction.

BEAR PARTS FOR SALE

The international trade in bear parts is another very serious threat to the bruins of the world. From backwoods Nova Scotia and Maine across the continent to

Early on a spring morning, an Ontario black bear prepares to pounce into a school of spawning suckers.

the coastal forests of British Columbia and Alaska, this illegal trade in bear gall bladders or ungdam, paws, penises, and other parts operates in much the same ruthless way as the international drug trade. According to Tom Shands, editor of *Bear News*, a periodical of the Great Bear Foundation, the increasing demand for bear parts is so great that there is a price tag on every remaining wild bear in the world.

The demand for bear parts is greatest in the Orient. Some of this demand is satisfied by suppliers in the Far East. For example, bear farms in China, Japan, and Korea produce some bear bile. On these "farms," incarcerated bears live painful, unnatural lives enclosed in small cages. Tubes inserted into the gall bladders drip bile that is collected and sold, much as a maple tree is tapped for syrup in New England.

But most gall bladder bile still comes from wild animals, which poachers slay simply to harvest their gall bladders. The profits from such activities are tremendous, and the risks are small. There are organized poaching rings and plenty of buyers, particularly in the western United States and Canada, who funnel the bear parts overseas, as well as to Asian communities in North America. The parts are used primarily in traditional medicine, but more recently in luxury shampoo. The paws are served as culinary delicacies. A few Taipei, Taiwan, restaurants serve bear paws for fifty dollars (U.S.) each. In North America, the trading is most brisk in areas where Asians have concentrated, such as British Columbia and California. In these regions, the traffickers seem better organized than the understaffed, underfunded law enforcement bureaus trying to stop them. The criminals operate out of seemingly legitimate businesses and storefronts, as well as in dark parking lots.

Ralph Krenz of British Columbia's Conservation Service has been following the bear parts traffic ever since the mid-1980s when wildlife officers discovered a hundred or more dead black bears, scattered across the province, with only paws and gall bladders removed. "Make no mistake," Krenz warns, "these people are criminals and dangerous. Combined with other threats facing bears today, they could cause our bear population to decline, even disappear, as they

have elsewhere in the world."

Investigators in California, often operating undercover, offer some chilling facts about the traders of bear parts. The illegal kill for parts is believed to equal the legitimate kill by hunters. One Korean buyer in the state purchased three hundred bear paws, fourteen bear gall bladders, and an indeterminate number of cougar gall bladders from professional hunting guides, who reported the buyer to authorities. Both legitimate guides and poachers as far east as Wisconsin have been approached by Asian buyers to sell any bear parts they can obtain.

But not all users of bear gall bladders and other parts are in the Orient. In 1987, investigators of poaching in the Great Smoky Mountains followed a trail that led to an eighty-two-year-old great-grandmother. She admitted that "for her health" she needed a wafer of dried gall bladder every day to go along with her dollop of corn likker.

Between 1986 and 1989, U.S. undercover agents paid over fifty thousand dollars to poachers for bear parts. As a result, fifty people were charged with over one thousand counts of illegal black bear killing. Albert Fellows of Sheffield, Massachusetts, who was operating a busy bear and whitetailed deer slaughterhouse in his barn, was charged with fifty-eight violations for selling paws, hides, and gall bladders.

The effect of such widespread poaching may be disastrous for the North American black bear. Dr. Edgard Espinosa, chief of the Forensics Laboratory of the U.S. Fish and Wildlife Service in Ashland, Oregon, offers a grim fact to an already horrifying discussion on bear part trading. All of the animal species used medicinally by Asian cultures—tigers, musk deer, Asian and sun bears, rhinos, snakes, tortoises, and sea turtles, for example—are now either endangered or extinct. The only exception, so far, is the North American black bear. So far.

CLEAR-CUTTING THE BEARS

Sadly, the garbage dumps of creeping suburbia and poaching for gall bladders are not the most serious of the problems faced by bears. You can see another grave danger near Hoonah, a small, native village on the north coast of Chichagof Island in southeastern Alaska, and a stronghold of coastal brown bears. You can stand on the shore of Port Frederick with Frank Wright, Jr., president of the native Tlingit-Haida Community Council, and he will point to the vistas stretching in virtually every direction, barren lands where clearcut logging has greatly depleted the once-endless forests. Clear-cutting continues where trees still stand, inexorably consuming this beautiful island and destroying his people's hunting grounds.

Clear-cutting means that no tree is left standing, and here the hairpin curves of logging roads wind among tree stumps that stretch to the horizon. Once this was bear habitat, but now it is desert. Native Americans do most of the timber cutting on the land owned by their Sealaska Corporation, but the destruction has been just as disgraceful on adjoining federal lands over much of southeastern Alaska. And it threatens to get worse. "Maybe," Alaskan environmentalist Mary Myer said to me recently, "they should just get all the bear gall bladders now, while they can. Soon no bears can live here anyway."

Researchers have long used culvert-trailer traps such as this one, baited, to capture (alive) bears for study and for release elsewhere. Three black bear cubs investigate this one; their mother has been lured inside.

THE TONGASS NATIONAL FOREST

The Tongass National Forest of southeastern Alaska is an extraordinary national treasure. It extends from Ketchikan in the south about five hundred miles (800 km) to Glacier Bay National Park in the north, covering seventeen million acres (6.8 million hectares) of coastal and inland rainforest, where yellow cedar, western hemlock, and Sitka spruce grow to the sky. In fact, it is the largest intact rainforest on earth. About one million acres (400,000 hectares) of this have been set aside by the U.S. Congress as wilderness under the Wilderness Act, which means the area cannot be logged or mined or "used," except for non-motorized recreation (including regulated hunting and fishing). Sitka blacktailed deer, coho, sockeye, and king salmon thrive here, and these species need this habitat as much as the native black and brown bears. The exquisitely green land attracts wilderness buffs and sea kayakers from around the world, and the land still provides the Tlingit and Haida people with a subsistence way of life many prefer. But far too much of the southeast Alaskan forest has already been cut—clear-cut—and the logs sold whole overseas, and now much of the Tongass is a wasteland. The soil erodes from the barren slopes, silting the rocky stream beds below, which were once prime salmon spawning streams. The worst may be yet to come.

In the U.S. Congress, where enemies of the American environment are not unusual, Senator Frank Murkowski of Alaska, a banker and large investor in the timber industry, may well be the worst example. As I write in late 1995, Senator Murkowski has introduced a bill that would open for logging an additional 645,000 acres (260,000 hectares) of the Tongass National Forest that is currently set aside for recreation and for Native American subsistence hunting and fishing. Logging roads, which break up intact forest, trigger erosion on steep hillsides, and allow easy access to pristine wilderness, would have to be built through wilderness areas and national parks. The bill would supersede laws that specifically prohibit such construction in these sanctuaries. Many of the beds of southeast Alaska's largest salmon-spawning runs, which are already in trouble, would be wiped out. We would also say goodbye to the bears, which would lose their forest habitat. For a long time the Tongass

Above: *Finding a territory of its own may be difficult for young grizzlies such as this because of ever-shrinking habitat and the spread of human development.*

Overleaf: *One of the most spectacular and sensitive wildlife sanctuaries on earth surrounds the McNeil River, Alaska, where these twin brown bear cubs are secure.*

has been treated more like a timber colony or a troublesome stepchild than a treasure.

The timber industry that Murkowski is playing up to does not acknowledge the impact these plans will have on the bears. Said simply, this is the greatest immediate threat to Alaskan bears, all Alaskan bears wherever they survive. Loss of habitat will destroy the Alaskan bear.

During my own lifetime, I have seen the great salmon fisheries of the Pacific coast, from California's Sacramento River northward to Washington, dwindle to nothing. The salmon in the lower forty-eight states are almost gone. They're disappearing in British Columbia and up into Alaska as well. Not too long ago

such a possibility would have been viewed by any rational person as ludicrous. For far too long the combination of politicians and too greedy fishermen—logging and overfishing—has been pushing salmon stocks to the brink of collapse.

Now some commercial fishermen may at last be seeing the light, and the end of their livelihood. Led by a trollers' association at Ketchikan, many Alaskan commercial fishermen are now opposing more large-scale logging, which, they say, will devastate many salmon runs. So are many local chambers of commerce, which realize that visitors seeking a wilderness experience, complete with bears, will not spend money to see vast, lifeless, eroding stumpfields.

Other Government-Subsidized Threats to the Environment

As a young man, I thought of our western range-lands as vast horizon-to-horizon plains of grass where cattle and cowboys roamed. It was a romantic and beautiful vision, but the reality today is much different. Widespread overgrazing is doing terrible, perhaps irreparable damage to 264 million acres (106 million hectares) of federal rangeland leased for grazing in the West. Even the Bureau of Land Management, a major custodian of these public lands, admits that more than two-thirds of its range is in unsatisfactory condition today. It is not far from the truth to say that a lot of our heritage is beginning to look like the rock-strewn deserts of the Middle East, where stock grazing has continued for thousands of years and not just a hundred years or less. Our General Accounting Office in Washington has concluded that some of these damaged rangelands could never really recover.

Destructive and unnecessary mining projects such as that proposed just northwest of Yellowstone could pollute entire watersheds and alter wilderness scenes such as this forever.

To add insult to grave injury, holders of grazing permits on Western lands—not struggling ranchers but, mainly, large corporations—pay the U.S. government only a fraction of what private landowners charge for grazing privileges. Some permit holders do not even graze their own stock; rather, they turn around and sublease to others at the going market price, making a tidy profit at our expense and pocketing money that rightly should go to the U.S. Treasury. For decades, various Secretaries of the Interior and conservation organizations such as the Wilderness Society have asked for higher grazing fees and greater protection for public rangelands. But every time, powerful livestock lobbyists have killed any such sensible ideas.

In addition to logging and ranching interests, subsidized mining threatens western lands. In 1872, President Ulysses S. Grant signed a general mining law, and ever since the government has been essentially giving away public land and precious minerals. The subsidies to mining companies have been particularly lavish, and even multinational corporations have been legally destroying our natural heritage, poisoning the land, and getting rich for over 125 years.

Consider especially one current example, which, if continued, could speed the Yellowstone grizzly bear's trip to oblivion. In 1994, Secretary of the Interior Bruce Babbitt was forced by the 1872 Mining Law to sell two thousand acres (800 hectares) of federal land to the Stillwater Mining Company, an international corporation. They paid ten thousand dollars for land believed to hold eight billion dollars—that's *billion*—in gold. The land also contains platinum and vanadium deposits worth thirty-two billion dollars, according to some geologists.

But far worse than the frightful loss of revenue, in my opinion, is the fact that this gold mine would be excavated less than two miles (3.2 km) from the northeastern boundary of Yellowstone National Park, where both bears and gray wolves, reintroduced in 1995, roam free. The mining company would plunder an estimated eight million tons (7.3 million metric tons) of ore from a mountain and excavate a seventy-seven-acre (31-hectare) lake ten stories deep to be filled with toxic waste. The operators guarantee that they will seal off the toxins from polluting three important, still-pure watersheds forever. But forever is a long time, especially if you happen to live in the affected area or if you have ever walked over the devastated lands left behind by other-mining ventures.

The bottom line is that the U.S. Congress should have rescinded the 1872 Mining Law long ago.

Above: *Denali National Park, Alaska, is one unspoiled wilderness where grizzlies have sufficient living space, as here along the Toklat River.*

Despite such efforts, the kow-towing to the timber industry is not likely to subside. In 1994 alone, the U.S. Forest Service wasted $265 million taxpayer dollars in its incredible, senseless eagerness to feed cheap logs to the timber industry or, even worse, to ship whole logs to Japan. We lost money on 109 of 120 sales of public timber (in bear habitat) in 1994. Still the timber industry wallows in such clout with your—our—senators and congressmen that the first forest-related action of 1995 was to authorize increased logging at the cheap subsidy rates, which will cost the government (and the taxpayer) $390 million while eliminating countless acres of precious wildlife habitat. It's a sickening thing to me.

What To Do About the Habitat Crisis

Bears and all the other wild creatures will roam free and prosper only as long as they have the environment in which to do it. Pointing out the problems is easy, but what should we do about them? Following are my suggestions.

To preserve our natural heritage, the first step is clear: We must stop paying private corporations to destroy public lands. All of us want government waste brought under control. We dream of lower taxes and recognize the grave need to reduce the national debt. To do this, the U.S. Congress proposes reducing aid to education, Medicare, and cutting school meals for poor children—everything except cutting their own budgets or the outrageous subsidies for corporate logging, mining, drilling, draining, and grazing of our parks, forests, and wildlife refuges. We simply must reform this monstrosity, and soon.

If we want to save our bears, which are an unfail-

Above: *Everywhere this adult grizzly bear roams, as here in central Alaska, it is the top of the food chain. But its future is in human hands.*

Facing page: *Grizzlies still roam in good numbers in the national parks of the beautiful Canadian Rockies. The scene here is of Bow Lake in Banff.*

ing index of the health of our land, we can begin by electing leaders, at all levels of government, whose primary interest is in the American environment and the future of the wilderness, not in their own reelections. After that we must press them, hound them without letup, to pass new laws and change old ones that lay waste to wilderness and squander billions of dollars to subsidize corporate profits.

It won't be easy, but it is not impossible.

Getting Along with Bears

On a dreary morning in September 1992, Mark Matheny and Fred Bahnson were bowhunting for elk and deer in Montana's Gallatin National Forest, just northwest of Yellowstone. Around noon, the two old buddies headed back toward their parked car a couple of miles away, when they suddenly flushed several ravens. Just beyond the raucous birds, Matheny spotted a silvery animal moving around to his left. It was a female grizzly bear with cubs, and they were feeding on a carcass.

According to Matheny, the bear came after them immediately. There were no trees to climb, so Matheny crouched down and held out his bow to try to defend himself. But the bear knocked him down and began to maul him.

Reacting as quickly as he could, Bahnson pulled out a can of pepper spray, which he had brought along in case of a bear attack, and squirted the bear. The bruin turned on him and knocked Bahnson down, sending his glasses and spray can flying on contact. Then the bear turned on Matheny again. Bahnson retrieved his pepper spray and squirted the bear until the can was empty. To return the favor, the bear bowled Bahnson over a second time. Then, as suddenly as it had attacked, the grizzly ran away with her cubs close behind. The two archers estimated the whole incident lasted fifteen or twenty seconds at most.

Bahnson, an ear, nose, and throat doctor, tended to his friend's severe cheek and scalp wounds, managing to stop the bleeding, and the two slowly walked the rest of the way to the car. Later, Matheny would need one hundred stitches to close his wounds. Both men survived.

There are two kinds of wild country in North America, with and without bears. A wise traveler in grizzly country will be doubly alert.

Matheny believes they were able to walk away from the attack and make it to a hospital because of the pepper spray. In fact, he is so convinced that it saved his life that today he manufactures and sells fifteen-ounce (445-ml) cans of concentrated pepper mist as a bear repellent, to be carried in a belt holster by hikers, campers, and hunters in bear country. Once inhaled, the main ingredient attacks the mucous membranes of the bear's nose, ears, and eyes with a powerful burning sensation. The discomfort lasts about ten minutes, and the spray does not cause permanent damage.

AVOIDING A BEAR SCARE

Throughout this book I have tried to emphasize that, although all bears should be regarded as potentially dangerous, only a very few of the most careless, most reckless, or least lucky of us will ever be attacked. We are far more likely to be mugged in a crowded shopping mall, injured in an automobile crash, or assaulted by a member of our immediate family than attacked by any kind of bear.

In Glacier National Park, where bear problems

Above: *A careless backpacker dropped or discarded this tuna can in Alaska, and a bear found it. Notice how easily it punctured the can to suck out the contents.*

Facing page: *Single hikers should be doubly watchful when walking in grizzly or brown bear country. It is really wiser and safer to travel with others.*

have generated a good deal of publicity, rangers have compiled statistics on fatal accidents since 1913. More than five times as many people (forty-eight) have died from drowning than from injuries in a grizzly bear attack (nine). Over the same period, forty-nine fatalities were attributed to mishaps while hiking and rock climbing, and thirteen people were killed by avalanches and falling rocks. Statistics also show that hypothermia, homicide, and falling from horses caused as many deaths as the bears.

The remote possibility of a bear encounter can be further reduced to practically zero if we always observe four vital rules: (1) never be careless with food in bear areas, (2) avoid mothers with cubs, (3) avoid surprising bears by coming upon them suddenly, and (4) never crowd or try to approach a bear. Mark Matheny was unfortunate enough to break two of the four rules. He surprised a mother with cubs feeding on a kill. Luckily, the final result was positive.

When you plan to hike in bear country, ask a ranger or other hikers in the region about recent bear activity. Visitor centers or ranger stations are good places to ask. In addition, national parks often close trails or post warnings for areas with frequent bear sightings. Hiking in a group helps avoid surprising bears—there are more eyes watching, and a group tends to make more noise than a single person. Also, bear attacks are most often on individuals and rarely on several people together. If you are alone (or even in a larger group), it may seem silly to talk in a loud voice, clap, whistle, sing, or make other noises to alert bears to your presence, but such behavior is prudent. It is also useful to learn to recognize bear signs, such as scat, claw marks on trees, and footprints. When you see signs of bears in the area, be especially watchful.

Campers, in particular, must be fastidious in bear country. Sleep in tents, not out in the open, no matter how fine the weather. Camp only in designated or fenced-in areas. Check out a prospective campsite carefully, and if there is bear sign or bear trails around it, go elsewhere. Total cleanliness is necessary to prevent smells that entice or excite bears; leave the smelly or greasy trail foods at home. Do not sleep in clothes worn while cooking and do not cook in or near the tents in which you will later sleep. Store food a good distance

from camp, suspended from a tree limb at least ten to twelve feet (3–4 m) above the ground. Plan, cook, and eat meals so that there are no leftovers. Never clean fish close to any camp. Leave scented deodorants, cosmetics, and soaps at home. Do not bring pets on camping trips; it may also be unwise to bring small children into bear areas. Children need to be under the closest supervision at all times. There is some evidence that a woman may be in more danger when backcountry camping during her menstrual period.

Feeding bears—deliberately or accidentally—is dangerous, and human food can also lead to major problems for the bears. Animals that beg for human food along roads often are hit by cars. Too often they eat foil and plastic wrappings, and these materials can damage a bear's digestive system. Unnatural human foods also can cause ulcers, tooth decay, and diseases we may yet know nothing about. Worst of all, human food is addictive and, once they've tasted it, most bears cannot get enough of it and will resort to any means to obtain more. As discussed earlier, a bear foraging near people can be captured and classified as a nuisance bear. If the bear continues to cause problems, wildlife biologists may be forced to kill the bear.

HOW CLOSE IS TOO CLOSE?

Photographers are especially tempted to move closer and closer to bears, in order to make that indistinct speck in the camera viewfinder into a much larger image. It is an urge I understand very well. But what exactly is "too close" to a bear?

The responses of all wild animals, even within the same species, differ greatly. No one can offer concrete limits for approaching or photographing bears in the wild. As long as a bear continues to behave normally— that is, does not nervously keep looking elsewhere and does not suddenly change direction or move steadily away—you are probably maintaining a safe distance. If the bear clicks its teeth or makes other mouth noises, holds its head low, swings its head from side to side, or acts in any way that seems aggressive, it is a signal to back off slowly.

Despite the best intentions and precautions, there will be times when a bear encounter seems inevitable. If you find yourself in such a situation, remain calm.

Few if any bears are really looking for trouble, and most that threaten or bluff will not actually attack. It is not a good idea to make sudden moves or to shout to scare off a grizzly, and there is disagreement whether direct, prolonged eye contact is provocative. If possible, give a bear plenty of room and never run. A bear is very likely to pursue you if you sprint away. Instead slowly back or detour away, keeping upwind if you can, so that the animal will not lose your scent and become confused. If unable to detour, look around for the nearest climbable tree and keep that tree in mind as you wait for the bear to move away, as it probably will.

In the rare occurrence when a bear does charge, your options are limited. Drop your backpack, coat, camera, or any other gear to decoy or delay the bear, and then climb at least twelve feet (3.7 m) into the stoutest tree available. As a last resort, assume a fetal or cannonball position, protecting your abdomen with legs and knees while tightly covering your head and face with your arms. Play dead. Most bears who attack people are not looking to kill for food, and they may walk away after teaching the "loser" a lesson.

Carrying a firearm such as a handgun is a possible security precaution when traveling in a wilderness inhabited by bears. In the hands of an unexcitable person with a lot of experience with guns, a gun might work very well. But for most a pistol is only an extra weight and a psychological crutch at best. Too many bear attacks come too suddenly to draw and use a gun. Firearms are not permitted in national parks and many other wildlife sanctuaries.

Bear behaviorists remain divided on the value of bear repellent sprays available on the market today such as the pepper spray described earlier. But more and more evidence points to the effectiveness of sprays that contain capsicum (a derivative of red peppers) as a main ingredient. In Yellowstone Park in 1988, a bear researcher who was charged by a grizzly sprayed the bear at point blank range with a red pepper solution. The bear still knocked him down and bit his leg, but the bruin then disappeared. It is difficult to say positively whether the spray made a difference, but Dick Knight, then leader of the Interagency Grizzly Bear Study Team, ordered the spray cans for all of his re-

Above: *A brown bear investigates a backpack discarded by frightened trekkers on a wilderness trail.*

Left: *Bear country in most national parks is well marked and regulations are posted along roads, trails, and in campgrounds.*

search team members. Alaska biologist John Hyde, natural history writer Terry Domico, and internationally known bear researcher Charles Jonkel are among the professionals who believe capsicum sprays can keep bears away if used properly.

Kananaskis Country is a two-thousand-square-mile (5,200-sq-km) recreation area south of Banff National Park and Calgary, Alberta, in the Canadian Rockies. Every summer more and more people hike and camp across this extremely scenic, rugged wilderness. It also happens to be prime grizzly bear coun-

try and, some say, a perfect setting for conflict. But so far there has not been the hint of a bear problem on the Country's 684 miles (1,100 km) of trails. This is probably the result of a most innovative approach, begun in 1982.

Stephen Herrero, a well-known environmental science professor, author of *Bear Attacks,* and bear-behavior authority at the University of Calgary, was commissioned to plan and lay out a network of backcountry trails that would be as bear-safe as they could be. Working with biologist Wayne McCrory, he

This mating pair of Alaskan brown bears (facing page) pauses briefly in their tryst to stare at a party of photographers. That's Peggy Bauer (above) *standing at the center of the group at Hallo Bay, with a 400mm telephotos lens and 35mm camera mounted on a tripod. Bob Mauck is kneeling; Mike Parks and Evelyn Mauck are at right.*

pinpointed the locations of the major bear feeding areas—berry patches, moist places with abundant green vegetation, streamsides—where the bears spend 90 percent of their time eating. Trails were then routed over open, higher ground, around these popular bear feeding areas and where visibility was very good. This bear-wary system, altered occasionally to suit changing conditions, has worked so well (without a single encounter) that it is being duplicated in Kokanee Glacier and Valhalla Provincial Parks in British Columbia, where bears also are numerous.

Herrero is convinced that hikers will be far safer on these carefully designed trails, but he admits that people are not his only concern. "The more humans are injured by bears," he notes, "the more likely it is that the bears will be destroyed." None of us wants

the destruction of bears, whether due to conflicts with people, poaching for parts, or the loss of habitat. With a little education and the will to keep enough land wild, we can coexist with these remarkable animals and remain safe in the wilderness.

This meeting may be too close for comfort. The authors were "shooting" a brown bear fishing in Hallo Bay when it suddenly turned around and kept coming in their direction, maybe just for a closer look at the pair of strange intruders. Photo © Robert Mauck.

Keeping Your Distance and Getting the Picture

Fortunately, it is possible with today's fine photographic equipment to shoot excellent photos, even closeups, without inviting aggression. Long telephoto lenses are the answer.

Very few of the bear photos you see in this book were made with lenses shorter than 400mm (or 8 power) attached to our 35mm single lens reflex cameras and mounted on tripods. Many were taken with a 600mm (or 12 power) telephoto, and some with a 1.4 tele-extender inserted between the camera and the lens, which converts the 600mm to an 840mm (or 17 power) lens. With this setup, I can clearly see the expression on a bear's face when it is half the length of a football field away. For a nonphotographer, the high-end binoculars and spotting scopes of today can bring a black or grizzly bear much closer to a bear watcher than even our powerful telephoto lenses.

Facing page: *Two hundred or so grizzlies still roam across Yellowstone Park. But only rarely nowadays does one of them give photographers such a fine portrait.*

Organizations

Black Bear Awareness, Inc.
P.O. Box 156
Trufant, MI 49347
(616) 984-2884

Black Bear Institute
145 West Conan Street
Ely, MN 55731
(218) 365-4480

Friends of McNeil River
P.O. Box 231091
Anchorage, AK 99523-1091
(907) 566-1533

Great Bear Foundation
Box 1289
Bozeman, MT 59771-1289
(406) 586-5533

Greater Yellowstone Coalition
P.O. Box 1874
Bozeman, MT 59771
(406) 586-1593

Grizzly Discovery Center
203 South Canyon
West Yellowstone, MT 59758
(800) 257-2570

North American Bear Center
1 East Chapman Street
Ely, MN 55731
(218) 365-6015

Yellowstone Grizzly Foundation
104 Hillside Court
Boulder, CO 80302
(303) 939-8126

References and Suggested Readings

Bamfield, A.W. F. *Mammals of Canada*. Toronto: University of Toronto Press, 1974.

Bauer, Erwin A. *Bear in their World*. New York: Outdoor Life Books, 1985.

Bauer, Erwin A. *Predators of North America*. New York: Outdoor Life Books, 1988.

Boone and Crockett Club. *Records of North American Big Game*, 10th ed. Helena, MT: Falcon Press, 1993.

Brown, David D. *The Grizzly in the Southwest*. Norman, OK: University of Oklahoma Press, 1985.

Burk, Dale, ed. *The Black Bear in Modern North America*. Clinton, NJ: Boone and Crockett Club/Amwell Press, 1979.

Craighead, Frank C., Jr. *Track of the Grizzly*. San Francisco: Sierra Club Books, 1979.

Domico, Terry and Mark Newman. *Bears of the World*. New York: Facts on File, 1988.

Dufresne, Frank. *No Room for Bears*. New York: Holt, Rinehart and Winston, 1965.

Ford, Barbara. *Black Bear: The Spirit of Wilderness*. Boston: Houghton Mifflin Co., 1981.

Herrero, Stephen. *Bear Attacks: Their Causes and Avoidance*. Piscataway, NJ: Winchester Press, 1985.

Laycock, George. *The Wild Bears*. New York: Outdoor Life Books, 1986.

McCracken, Harold. *The Beast That Walks Like Man*. Garden City, NY: Hanover House, 1955.

Miller, S., N. Barichello, and D. Tate. *The Grizzly Bear of the Mackenzie Mountains, Northwest Territories*. Yellowknife, NWT: NWT Dept. of Renewable Resources Completion Report No. 3, 1981.

Murie, Adolph. *The Grizzlies of Mount McKinley*. Seattle: University of Washington, 1981.

Rue, L. L., III. *Furbearing Animals of North America*. New York: Crown, 1981.

Russell, Andy. *Grizzly Country*. New York: Ballantine Books, 1967.

Russell, Charles. *Spirit Bear*. Toronto: Key Porter, 1994.

Storer, Tracy I. and Lloyd P. Tevis, Jr. *California Grizzly*. Lincoln, NE: University of Nebraska Press, 1978.

Walker, Tom and Larry Aumiller. *River of Bears*. Stillwater, MN: Voyageur Press, 1993.

Ward, Kennan. *Grizzlies in the Wild*. Minocqua, WI: Northword Press, 1994.

Overleaf: *It is the height of summer and a Montana grizzly looks out on its beautiful, green, but shrinking world.*

Index

About the Authors

Photo © Brent Allen

Erwin and Peggy Bauer are busy, full-time photographers and writers of travel, adventure, and environmental subjects. Based in Paradise Valley, Montana, the Bauers have specialized in photographing wildlife worldwide for over forty years. Their images come from the Arctic to the Antarctic, Borneo to Brazil, Africa to India, Madagascar to Malaysia, and beyond.

Erwin and Peggy Bauer may be the most frequently published wildlife photographers in the world today. The Bauers' recent magazine credits include *Natural History, Outdoor Life, Audubon, National Geographic, Smithsonian, Wildlife Conservation, National Wildlife* and *International Wildlife, Sierra, Safari, Chevron USA,* and *Nature Conservancy.* Their photographs annually illustrate the calendars of Voyageur Press, the Sierra Club, the Audubon Society, World Wildlife Fund, and others. The Bauers have more than a dozen books currently in print, including *Yellowstone, Whitetails, Mule Deer, Antlers: Nature's Majestic Crown,* and *Elk,* all published by Voyageur Press. The couple has won many awards for wildlife photography in national and international photographic competitions.

Overleaf: *Before claw-marking a tree, a female grizzly looks back over its trail to see her two cubs are still following.*